REACHING THE LOST

Colin Dye

Sovereign World

Sovereign World Ltd
PO Box 777
Tonbridge
Kent TN11 0ZS
England

Scriptural quotations are from the New King James Version, Thomas Nelson Inc., 1991.

ISBN 1 85240 207 5

This Sovereign World book is distributed in North America by Renew Books, a ministry of Gospel Light, Ventura, California, USA. For a free catalog of resources from Renew Books/Gospel Light, please contact your Christian supplier or call 1-800-4-GOSPEL.

Typeset by CRB Associates, Reepham, Norfolk
Printed in England by Clays Ltd, St Ives plc.

FOREWORD

The material in this *Sword of the Spirit* series has been developed over the past ten years at Kensington Temple in London as we have sought to train leaders for the hundreds of churches and groups we have established. Much of the material was initially prepared for the students who attend the International Bible Institute of London – which is based at our church.

Over the years, other churches and colleges have asked if they may use some of our material to help them establish training courses for leaders in their towns and countries. This series has been put together partly to meet this growing need, as churches everywhere seek to train large numbers of new leaders to serve the growth that God is giving.

The material has been constantly refined – by myself, by the students as they have responded, by my many associate pastors, and by the staff at the Bible Institute. In particular, my colleague Timothy Pain has been responsible for sharpening, developing and shaping my different courses and notes into this coherent series.

I hope that many people will use this series in association with our developing Satellite Bible School, but I also pray that churches around the world will use the books to train leaders.

We live at a time when increasing numbers of new churches are being started, and I am sure that we will see even more startling growth in the next few decades. It is vital that we re-examine the way we train and release leaders so that these new churches have the best possible biblical foundation. This series is our contribution to equipping tomorrow's leaders with the eternal truths that they need.

Colin Dye

CONTENTS

INTRODUCTION

Mission is the true church's greatest passion and purpose. As every fire exists to burn, so every congregation should be a holy conflagration reaching out to the people around them with God's infinite grace and love. Every church must spread the gospel, or suppress in shame; obey the Great Commission, or pretend that it is nothing to do with them; reach the lost, or leave them to perish. There is no middle way.

God has entrusted us with a burning mission to speak his message of total forgiveness in words that people can understand, to demonstrate his compassionate power in deeds that people can see, and to incarnate his life-giving gospel with lives which dazzle people with his holiness.

Nobody pretends that this is easy – we know that it cost Jesus his life, and that the missionary church has always faced a mixture of apathy and opposition. There will always be some people who do not want to hear a word about Jesus, while others will seek to dampen our fire and gag our mouths.

In the last fifty years, there have been thousands of conferences, courses, books and videos on evangelism – yet the church is still inactive and the world largely unreached. When the task is so urgent and the need so great, it almost seems wrong to ask anyone to make time to study evangelism. But the church will not recover its passion for mission until it has asked and answered some very basic questions.

Are people truly lost? Does God care individually about all the 6,000 million people alive today? Is the gospel genuinely *good* news? Can people's natures be changed? Did Jesus' death actually make a difference? Did he literally rise from the dead? Will all people really be judged by him one day? If the answer to these questions is a reasoned 'Yes', mission or evangelism is the only sensible conclusion.

This is a book for believers who are willing to set aside their own ideas about evangelism, and are eager to study God's Word to discover his revelation about our mission. We need to learn what the Scriptures teach about the lost, what they reveal about the good news itself, and how they show the church reaching the lost with the gospel.

Please make sure that you read each scriptural reference – and tick the margin reference boxes as you go along to show that you have. Answer every question and think through each point as it is made. Before moving on to a new section, think carefully about the implications of what you have studied. Please allow God to speak to you about your personal evangelism as you study his word.

At the end of the book, there is some activity material and questions. Please make sure that you study Parts 1–9 before beginning to work through the activities, as this will ensure that you have an overview of the biblical teaching about evangelism before you try to apply the details of any one area. These questions will help you to grasp and apply the scriptural material that you have studied.

You will also be able to use the activity pages when you teach the material to small groups. Please feel free to photocopy these pages and distribute them to any group you are leading. Although you should work through all the questions when you are studying on your own, please don't expect a small group to cover all the material. Instead, prayerfully select those parts that you think are most relevant for your group. This means that, at some meetings you might use all the material whilst at others you might use only a small part.

By the time you finish this book, it is my prayer that you will have a much better understanding of God's purpose in sending us into his world with his gospel, the different ways that we should spread the gospel, and the resources which he has given to equip us for this task. In particular, I pray that you will be so convinced by the truth of the gospel, so equipped with the power of the Spirit, and so motivated by the love of the Father, that you will start to reach the lost and hurting people around you with gospel effectiveness.

Colin Dye

PART ONE

evangelism

This eighth book in the *Sword of the Spirit* series is about *biblical evangelism*. It is called *Reaching the Lost*, however, because many believers seem not to realise what evangelism fully means. They appear to limit their understanding to big crusades, tract distribution, tv preachers and knocking on doors; they seem not to appreciate the depth, breadth and kaleidoscopic variety of New Testament mission.

Some believers seem to think that evangelism is best left to specialist evangelists; while others appear to confuse it with evangelicalism – they identify the act of spreading the good news with the ideas of one tradition within the church. If, however, we are concerned to reach the lost in the way that God intends, we need to understand what he has revealed in the Scriptures about the ministry of evangelism.

What is evangelism?

In the last eighty years, there has been considerable debate and discussion about the meaning of 'evangelism'. Several important definitions have been suggested, each with a slightly different emphasis.

In 1918, the Archbishops' Committee of Enquiry on the evangelistic work of the Church of England decided that: 'to evangelise is
so to present Jesus Christ in the power of the Holy Spirit, that men
shall come to put their trust in God through him, to accept him as
their Saviour, and serve him as their King in the Fellowship of his
Church'.

This famous definition helpfully stresses that evangelism involves:

- *declaring a specific message*
- *depending on the Holy Spirit*
- *presenting Jesus as the Christ*
- *demanding discipleship*

It also suggests, however, that the essence of evangelism is
producing converts.

Leaders who emphasise God's sovereignty disagree. They argue
that evangelism is our human responsibility, whereas only God gives
faith and creates new life. They acknowledge that evangelism points
people towards trusting God, but they insist that it is the Spirit who
enables people to trust God. We consider this in *Salvation by Grace.*

These leaders argue that evangelism should not be defined by results
or measured by conversions; they say that it should be understood as *a
work of proclamation* which aims to achieve or facilitate conversions.
Most of them stress the priority of preaching, and define evangelism
as: 'proclaiming Jesus Christ to sinful people in order that, through the
power of the Spirit, they may come to trust God through him'.

In fact, some influential evangelical groups insist that the word
evangelism should be restricted in meaning to *proclaiming the message
of salvation.*

Church leaders from other Christian traditions criticise this
evangelical emphasis on proclamation. They agree that preaching is
an important part of evangelism; but orthodox leaders insist that the
church's presence in the world, its holy *living and serving*, is equally
indispensable; while pentecostal leaders maintain that supernatural
signs and wonders must accompany preaching.

These basic ideas about evangelism can help us to understand the
different emphases of other church groups, but we must turn to the
Scriptures if we are to grasp the real meaning of biblical evangelism.

The New Testament uses two groups of Greek words to describe what Christians call 'evangelism'. Many of the disagreements about evangelism stem from misunderstandings about the meanings of these two important groups of words – and from an over-emphasis on one or other of them.

GOOD NEWS

The first group of New Testament words is based around the Greek noun *euangelion*. This comes from the two Greek words *eu*, 'well' or 'noble' and *angelia*, 'message' or 'tidings'; so *euangelion* means 'the good news', 'the glad tidings', or 'the noble message'. The common word 'gospel' is simply the Old English way of spelling 'good-speak'.

This immediately establishes that evangelism is inseparably linked with the gospel, with the good news. We can say that anything which relates to the gospel must relate to evangelism, and that anything which does not relate to the gospel does not relate to evangelism.

The related Greek noun *euangelistes* is also used in the New Testament. This comes from *eu*, 'well' and *angelos*, 'messenger', and literally means 'a messenger of good'. The English word 'evangelist' is simply a transliteration of *euangelistes*.

The Greek word *euangelizo* is the verbal form of *euangelion*, and is almost impossible to translate neatly into modern English.

In *Living Faith*, we see that the noun *pistis* and the verb *pisteuo* are different forms of one word and express identical ideas. If English were a logical language, these would be translated as 'faith' and 'to faith', so that their association were clear. Instead, we say 'to believe' or 'to put faith in' when 'to faith' would be clearer, simpler and more accurate.

The same problem arises with *euangelion* and *euangelizo*. Instead of saying 'to gospel', the English language forces us to invent a verb to place before the noun 'gospel'. Different translators of the Bible choose different verbs, and the word they use inevitably reflects their theological outlook. Most select 'to preach the gospel', or 'to announce the good news', or 'to bring glad tidings'. In literal Greek, however, it is all 'to gospel', or 'to good news', or 'to evangelise'.

Most evangelical Bible translators render *euangelizo* as 'to preach the gospel' or 'to proclaim the gospel': some believers then point to this as proof that preaching is the essence of evangelism!

Other church leaders argue that we could also render *euangelizo* as 'to be the gospel' or 'to demonstrate the gospel'. In fact, a more neutral verb like 'to spread', 'to bring' or 'to bear' would be better.

We must recognise, however, that the extra verb is absent in the New Testament, and we must ensure we do not think that evangelism is essentially 'proclamation', or 'incarnation', or 'demonstration' just because 'to gospel' is not an acceptable English verb!

We can think about this group of words in the following ways.

Greek word	transliteration	literal translation	good translation
euangelion	the evangel	the good news	the gospel
euangelizo	to evangelise	to good news	to bring the gospel
euangelistes	an evangelist	a good newser	a gospel messenger

Modern Christians increasingly use the verb 'to evangelise', and it would make sense to use this transliteration of *euangelizo* in the New Testament itself – especially as *euangelistes* is always transliterated as 'evangelist'. But we should start to use 'evangelise' only when we know fully what the Bible teaches about it.

Remember, our understanding of evangelism must be based in the way that the New Testament uses the *euangelion* group of words, and not in human ideas or church traditions.

To evangelise

The Greek verb *euangelizo* appears about 50 times in the New Testament. It is used, for example, in Luke 4:18, 43; 7:22; 9:6; 20:1; Acts 8:4, 25, 35; 14:15, 21; 15:35; Romans 10:15; 15:20; 1 Corinthians 1:17; 9:16; 15:1–2; 2 Corinthians 10:16; 11:7; Galatians 1:11, 16; 4:13; Ephesians 3:8; Hebrews 4:2, 6; 1 Peter 1:12, 25 and 4:6.

Luke 4:18–19 is particularly illuminating. This is one of Jesus' most important statements, and we can think of it as his 'manifesto' or 'mission statement'. In this passage, Jesus summarises the purpose of his anointing as proclaiming/preaching/bearing/bringing/spreading good news to the poor. In truth, he was anointed with the Spirit 'to evangelise the poor'.

Luke 4:18–19 ☐

Although most English translations use the one word 'preach' three times in these verses, two Greek words are used. *Euangelizo* is used in the first clause, but a different word – *kerusso* (which is best translated as 'herald' or 'proclaim') – is used in the fourth and seventh clauses.

Jesus then provides five examples of what 'evangelising the poor' means in practice: this is his definition of spirit-anointed evangelism. We can say that, according to Jesus, biblical evangelism includes:

- *healing the broken-hearted*

- *liberating the captives*

- *restoring sight to the blind*

- *releasing the oppressed*

- *proclaiming God's message of freedom and favour*

Jesus was not sent from the Father, and anointed with the Spirit, just to preach sermons in Jewish synagogues. Rather, he came to reveal God through words, through deeds and through a perfect life; and he came to do this in a way which was particularly relevant to the poor – the Greek word *ptochos* means 'the afflicted' or 'the hurting'.

This idea is repeated in Luke 7:18–22. John the Baptist wanted to know whether Jesus was the Messiah or not, and sent two disciples to ask him. Verse 21 describes Jesus' active response to their questions; and verse 22 records his message to John: 'Go and tell John the things you have *seen* and *heard*: that the blind see, the lame walk, the lepers are cleansed, the deaf hear, the dead are raised, the poor have the gospel preached to them.'

Luke 7:18–22 ☐

This is very similar to Jesus' self-announcement in Luke 4:18. First, he lists the aspects of his Spirit-anointed evangelistic mission; then he summarises his anointed purpose as, 'the poor (the afflicted or hurting) have the gospel brought/announced/spread/borne/proclaimed to them' – *the hurting have been evangelised.*

This principle is underlined again in Luke 8. Most English versions of verse one describe Jesus as 'preaching and bringing the glad tidings' to every city and village in the area. This gives translators a problem. Luke reports that Jesus '*kerusson* and *euangelizmenos*': it is plain, therefore, that these are different activities. If those translators who render *euangelizo* 'preach the gospel' were to be consistent, they would have to state that Jesus 'preached and preached'! In fact, 'preaching' is not even an accurate translation of *kerusson*, for it points to a herald's indiscriminate proclamation of his master's fixed message.

Luke 8:1 ☐

Luke 8:1 is conclusive proof that evangelism is not just a verbal action. Proclamation and evangelism must go hand-in-hand, but they are not the same thing.

Luke 8:2–56 ☐

Luke 8:2–56 appears to be Luke's exposition of 8:1. He makes a general statement in verse one; then he illustrates this statement throughout the rest of the chapter. We see that Jesus:

- *preached and answered questions* – verse 4–18

- *brought peace to the terrified* – verse 22–25

- *liberated the captives* – verse 26–39

- *healed the sick* – verse 43–48

- *raised the dead* – verse 49–56

If, as Luke 8:1 implies, proclamation and evangelising are different, it seems likely that the miracles in 22–56 illustrate Jesus' evangelising – for the parables in 4–18, clearly illustrate his proclaiming.

And if 'to evangelise' is 'to bear, bring or spread good news', the Luke 8 miracles were a tremendously effective way of doing this. These miracles were not preparation for evangelism, nor were they consequences of evangelism – they were in themselves evangelism.

Romans 15:18–20 ☐

The apostle Paul makes the same point in Romans 15:18–20. Most translations refer to preaching in verses 19 and 20, but these words are absent in Greek. What Paul literally writes in verse 19 is, 'I have filled the gospel of Christ'; and, in verse 20, 'I have made it my aim to evangelise'.

Verses 18–19 show how Paul had 'filled the gospel' and 'gospelled' – how he had evangelised: it was in words and deeds, in mighty signs and wonders by the power of the Spirit.

Mark starts his account of Jesus' ministry by referring in the first verse to the *euangelion* – to the good news of Jesus. He then sets the scene by recording a typical day in Jesus' life. Verses 21–34 show that, on one Sabbath day, Jesus' gospelling, or evangelising, includes:

- *preaching in the synagogue* – verse 21–22

- *delivering a captive* – verse 23–26

- *healing the sick* – verse 29–31, 34

- *casting out demons* – verse 34

On through Mark, and through every 'Gospel', we see that Jesus announced good news through preaching, teaching and one-to-one conversations; that he demonstrated good news through mighty signs and wonders; and that he lived good news by accepting, receiving, embracing and forgiving the afflicted and hurting people of his day.

It is the same in the early church. Acts 8:1 describes the scattering of the persecuted disciples throughout Judea and Samaria, and 8:4 shows that they went everywhere 'evangelising'.

Acts 8:5–13 illustrates this evangelism with the story of Philip. It reports that his evangelism included:

- *preaching* – verse 5

- *miracles* – verse 6

- *casting out demons* – verse 7

- *healing the sick* – verse 8

Acts 8:12 then summarises Philip's activity by saying that the Samaritans believed as he *euangelizomenoi* – as he evangelised. It is little wonder that Acts 21:8 describes Philip as an 'evangelist'.

It is the same in Acts 10:36–38. First, Peter describes Jesus as 'the Word', the 'Lord of all', who was sent to Israel *euangelizomenos* – evangelising. Next, Peter repeats Jesus' Luke 4:18 principle and relates his evangelising to his anointing. Then, he reports that Jesus' evangelism included:

- *proclamation* – verse 37

- *doing good* – verse 38

- *healing the oppressed* – verse 38

Mark 1:1 ☐
1:21–34 ☐

Acts 8:1–4 ☐
8:5–13 ☐

Acts 21:8 ☐

Acts 10:36–38 ☐

This scriptural material should convince us that evangelism does not consist entirely of preaching: true biblical evangelism includes the *verbal proclamation* of the good news, but it must also include the *visual demonstration* of the good news in signs, wonders, peace and good deeds. It is reaching the lost, not just preaching to the lost.

The evangel

The noun *euangelion* appears almost eighty times in the New Testament. In almost every instance, it is linked with another word which describes the originator of the message, or the content of the message, or the purpose of the message.

It is, for example,

- *the gospel of the kingdom* – Matthew 4:23; 9:35; 24:14

- *the gospel of God* – Mark 1:14; Romans 1:1; 15:16; 2 Corinthians 11:7; 1 Thessalonians 2:2, 9; 1 Peter 4:17

- *the gospel of God concerning his Son* – Romans 1:1–3

- *the gospel of his Son* – Romans 1:9

- *the gospel of Jesus Christ, the Son of God* – Mark 1:1

- *the gospel of our Lord Jesus* – 2 Thessalonians 1:8

- *the gospel of Christ* – Romans 15:19

- *the gospel of the glory of Christ* – 2 Corinthians 4:4

- *the gospel of the grace of God* – Acts 20:24

- *the gospel of the glory of the blessed God* – 1 Timothy 1:11

- *the gospel of your salvation* – Ephesians 1:13

- *the gospel of peace* – Ephesians 6:15

- *the eternal gospel* – Revelation 14:6

- *my gospel* – Romans 2:16; 16:25; 2 Timothy 2:8

- *our gospel* – 2 Corinthians 4:3; 1 Thessalonians 1:5; 2 Thessalonians 2:14

From these passages, we learn four basic truths about the message that we are called to bear in biblical evangelism.

1. *it is the gospel of the kingdom*

In this *Sword of the Spirit* series, we study the kingdom in *The Rule of God*. We establish that the kingdom refers to 'the kingly rule and reign of God'; that it is both 'now and not yet'; and that God rules 'personally, in-and-through Christ; rather than through the Law'.

The personal rule of God came with Jesus, which means that the kingdom is here because he is here.

It is significant that the first reference to the 'gospel of the kingdom' is set in the context of spoken proclamation *and* healing the sick *and* casting out evil spirits; and that the second reference is set in the context of spoken proclamation *and* healing *and* unusual compassion. We see this in Matthew 4:23–24 and 9:35–36.

Matthew
4:23–24 ☐
9:35–36 ☐

The gospel of the kingdom is the good news that God's rule is now present in person; and that he rules over people, over sickness, over evil, over everything.

Every aspect of God's rule is announced in words, demonstrated in deeds and manifested in compassion. If the gospel we bear is not all of these, it is not really biblical good news.

2. *it is the gospel of God*

The gospel of God is good news *about* God. It is the wonderful news about the grace-initiating Father that we examine in *Knowing the Father*. It is the amazing message of divine revelation and human redemption that we consider in *Salvation by Grace*. It is the life-giving story of the eternally-submitting Son that we study in *Knowing the Son*. And it is the empowering truths about the enabling, self-effacing Spirit that we discover in *Knowing the Spirit*.

The gospel is not just good news about Jesus; it is also good news about the Father and good news about the Spirit. It is the gospel about the full triune God.

The gospel of God, however, is also good news *from* God. It is all his initiative, his revelation – God has spoken his truths about himself.

As we see in *Living Faith* and *Listening to God*, every word from God is always a self-revelation of God; so the gospel of God is his good news about himself – the full triune God.

Galatians 1:6–9 ☐

2 Corinthians
            11:4 ☐

This means that we must take great care not to twist or alter the gospel in any way. Galatians 1:6–9 and 2 Corinthians 11:4 underline the seriousness of this.

3.   *it is the gospel of Jesus Christ*

The gospel of Jesus is the good news that *he brought into the world*. Without his ministry, there would be no forgiveness, no life, no freedom, no hope; without him, humanity would remain alienated from God, bound by Satan, wracked by guilt and spiritually dead; without his gospel-bearing activity, there simply would be no good news.

But the gospel of Jesus is also the good news that *he embodied in the world*. The incarnation is the heart of the gospel. God did not speak a message in heaven, he lived a life on earth. And God did not just send a message from heaven, for the Word became flesh and God's perfect way of living was seen on earth. Without Jesus' gospel-embodying life, there would be no good news.

John 14:9 ☐

In one sense, we can say that evangelism which consists only of spoken proclamation is almost a denial of the gospel – for incarnation is both the content and the embodiment, the Word and the flesh, the message and the means, of good news. John 14:9 teaches that we know the truth about God because we *see* the truth in Jesus' life.

4.   *it is a personal gospel*

The New Testament speaks about 'my gospel' and 'our gospel'. It is a message that we are meant to appropriate personally – to the extent that it becomes *our* gospel almost as much as it is *his* gospel.

By using many different verbs with *euangelion*, the New Testament makes it clear how we should and should not respond to the gospel. For example we can:

Mark 1:15 ☐
        8:35 ☐
Romans 1:1 ☐
        1:9 ☐
        1:16 ☐

- *believe the gospel* – Mark 1:15

- *lose our lives for the gospel* – Mark 8:35

- *be separated to the gospel* – Romans 1:1

- *serve in the gospel* – Romans 1:9

- *be ashamed of the gospel* – Romans 1:16

- *obey the gospel* – Romans 10:16

- *minister the gospel* – Romans 15:16

- *hinder the gospel* – 1 Corinthians 9:12

- *receive the gospel* – 2 Corinthians 11:4

- *fellowship in the gospel* – Philippians 1:5

- *labour in the gospel* – Philippians 4:3

- *suffer hardship in the gospel* – 2 Timothy 1:8

The New Testament also uses several different verbs to describe how we spread the gospel. For example, we can:

- *preach the gospel* – Matthew 4:23; Galatians 2:2

- *speak the gospel* – 1 Thessalonians 2:2

- *testify to the gospel* – Acts 20:24

- *evangelise the gospel* – 1 Corinthians 15:1; 2 Corinthians 11:7; Galatians 1:11

- *proclaim the gospel* – 1 Corinthians 9:14

This rich biblical language suggests that we are called to be deeply committed to the gospel *and* firmly dedicated to spreading the gospel.

The evangelist

The noun *euangelistes* is used only three times in the New Testament – in Acts 21:8; Ephesians 4:11 and 2 Timothy 4:5.

We have seen that *euangelistes* means a messenger of the gospel, and have noted that Acts 21:8 identifies Philip as an evangelist because he spread the gospel through words *and* deeds, through proclamation *and* demonstration.

Interestingly, Paul's command in 2 Timothy 4:5 to 'do the work of an evangelist' follows his command in 4:2–4 to 'preach the word'. This shows that 'preaching' and 'evangelism' are not the same activity, and that evangelistic preaching is not all there is to preaching.

Ephesians 4:11 shows that the evangelistic ministry is functionally distinct within the church, and that an evangelist's primary purpose

Romans 10:16 ☐
15:16 ☐

1 Corinthians
9:12 ☐

2 Corinthians
11:4 ☐

Philippians 1:5 ☐
4:3 ☐

2 Timothy 1:8 ☐

Matthew 4:23 ☐

Galatians 2:2 ☐

1 Thessalonians
2:2 ☐

Acts 20:24 ☐

1 Corinthians
15:1 ☐

2 Corinthians
11:7 ☐

Galatians 1:11 ☐

1 Corinthians
9:14 ☐

Acts 21:8 ☐

Ephesians 4:11 ☐

2 Timothy 4:2–5 ☐

is 'the equipping of the saints for the work of ministry, for the edifying of the body of Christ'. We consider this in *Glory in the Church*.

Evangelism

It should be plain that our thinking about biblical evangelism should be based in the New Testament use of the *euangelion* group of words. And it should be equally clear that biblical evangelism involves:

- *proclamation* – preaching, testifying, speaking, proclaiming, debating, announcing, answering questions, etc.

- *demonstration* – healing the sick and broken-hearted, releasing the bound, casting out demons, signs, wonders, miracles, etc.

- *incarnation* – living God's life among the afflicted and hurting, feeling God's compassion, suffering hardship, being ready to lose our lives, etc.

In particular, we have seen that biblical evangelism has a particular focus on the *ptochos*. Most translations of the Bible render this as 'the poor', but it literally means 'someone who is cowering down or hiding in fear'. A few modern versions reflect this by translating *ptochos* as 'the afflicted', and we can best appreciate this today by thinking in terms of 'the hurting' rather than 'the poor'.

This means that truly Christ-like evangelism does not focus on reaching those who have few material or financial resources; rather, it concentrates on reaching those who are afflicted and hurting, on the broken-hearted, the blind, the imprisoned, the oppressed; in fact, on reaching all those men and women who have been hurt in some way by sin, by Satan and by society's actions and attitudes.

HERALD

Most Christian thinking about evangelism is also shaped by a second group of New Testament words. These are based around the Greek noun *kerux* – which means 'a herald'.

A herald

Kerux is used only three times in the New Testament, in 1 Timothy 2:7; 2 Timothy 1:11 and 2 Peter 2:5, and is usually translated as 'preacher'. Today, however, the common idea of a preacher is quite different from that of a herald.

1 Timothy 2:7 ☐
2 Timothy 1:11 ☐
2 Peter 2:5 ☐

The essence of heralds (and, therefore, of all words in the *kerux* group) is that they travel from place to place, announcing a message which has been given to them by their king, and announcing it publicly to whoever they meet.

We tend to think of a preacher, however, as someone who gives a doctrinal address, which they have carefully constructed, to a closed group of convinced believers in a church building. This is the exact opposite of a herald!

Heralds do not have to be learned or clever, and they do not have to be trained or experienced; they merely have to be trustworthy and reliable. They do not express their own ideas; they simply pass on the king's message. And they do not offer their personal opinions; they proclaim only what the king has told them to say. On their own, heralds are nothing; their significance lies only in their representation of the one who has sent them.

In 1 Timothy 2:7 and 2 Timothy 1:11, Paul describes himself as a herald, an apostle and a teacher. By using these words in a linked sequence, Paul shows that they are both linked and distinct.

For example, a herald/preacher is distinct from a teacher, and heralding/preaching is distinct from teaching. The herald/preacher delivers a message indiscriminately; whereas a teacher instructs only those who want to learn and who choose to listen.

Yet heralds are related to apostles and teachers in that they are all 'sent'. A herald is sent by the king with the king's message; the Greek word *apostolos* literally means 'one who is sent'; and Paul makes it clear that he has been sent as a teacher to a specific group of people.

In these passages, Paul uses the three words in a sequential format. First, he is sent to the Gentiles as a herald: he bears the king's message – the good news – and announces it publicly to everyone he meets. Next, he is sent as an apostle to those who believe the king's message and act on it: he forms them into a church – into a functioning group of the king's people. And then he is sent to teach those who want to learn the king's ways. We consider this in *Glory in the Church*.

To herald

The Greek verb *kerusso* is derived from *kerux*. It means 'to herald' or 'to act as a herald', but is usually translated in the New Testament as 'to preach' or 'to proclaim'. As we have seen, preaching no longer communicates accurately the meaning of the *kerux* word group.

Kerusso is used about sixty times in the New Testament, and its literal meaning is clear in Mark 1:45; Luke 12:3 and Revelation 5:2. By definition, *kerusso* always implies three things:

- *a personal commissioning as a herald for a particular group of people*: for example, Mark 3:14; 16:15–20; Luke 9:2; Acts 10:42

- *a specific message from the king*: for example, Matthew 4:23; 9:35; 10:7; 24:14; Mark 1:14; 16:15; Luke 4:19; 8:1; 9:2; Acts 8:5; 9:20; 20:25; 28:31; Romans 10:8; 1 Corinthians 9:27; 15:12; 2 Corinthians 1:19; 1 Thessalonians 2:9

- *obedience to the commission and the message*: for example, Matthew 11:1; Mark 1:39; 6:12; Acts 8:5; 9:20; 1 Corinthians 15:11; Galatians 2:2

These passages show that *kerusso* is often linked with *euangelion*. The king's heralds are sent essentially to proclaim his 'gospel', the good news from-and-about the king.

We see this, for example, in Matthew 24:14; Mark 13:10; 14:9; 16:15, 20; Luke 8:1; 9:2; 24:47; Acts 8:5; 19:13; 28:31; Romans 10:14–15; 1 Corinthians 1:23; 15:11–12; 2 Corinthians 1:19; 4:5; 11:4; Galatians 2:2; Philippians 1:15; Colossians 1:23 and 1 Thessalonians 2:9.

As we have noted, however, the spoken proclamation of the herald's message is only one aspect of evangelism. It is an important part, but it must complement a demonstration and an incarnation of the gospel.

The herald's message

The noun *kerugma* refers to the heralds' message, and tends to be translated as 'preaching'. It always points to *the content* of the heralds' proclamation rather than to their act of proclaiming. And it means a distinct and delineated message which the heralds have been given by the king, rather than a message which they have composed or adjusted themselves.

Kerugma is used in the New Testament in Matthew 12:41; Luke 11:32; Romans 16:25; 1 Corinthians 1:21; 2:4; 15:14; 2 Timothy 4:17 and Titus 1:3.

Because *kerugma* literally means a fixed message, theologians and church leaders have debated strongly whether or not the early church evangelistic preaching contained a fixed *kerugma*.

Some leaders argue that the *kerugma* was a fixed series of factual statements about Christ's life and ministry, which culminated in a demand for repentance and faith. While others maintain that the *kerugma* was simply a presentation of a personal encounter with the living Lord Jesus.

In fact, the early church *kerugma* seems to have been *both* a message which was rooted in the historical facts of Jesus' life, death, resurrection and ascension, *and* an introduction to the living Christ who had risen from the dead. We see this, for example, in 1 Corinthians 1:23 and 15:14. We consider the content of the heralds' message in detail in Part Six.

Evangelism

As we go through this book, we will keep on referring to 'evangelism'. It is vital we start to understand this in terms of the way that the *euangelion* and the *kerux* group of words are both used in the New Testament.

By now, we should appreciate that biblical evangelism depends on the anointing with the Spirit, focuses on the hurting and involves a demonstration of the gospel in signs and wonders, an incarnation of the gospel in compassion and holiness, and a public, herald-like, proclamation of the king's good message to everyone that we meet.

Matthew 12:41 ☐

Luke 11:32 ☐

Romans 16:25 ☐

1 Corinthians
1:21 ☐
2:4 ☐
15:14 ☐

2 Timothy 4:17 ☐

Titus 1:3 ☐

1 Corinthians
1:23 ☐

PART TWO

the lost

Matthew 9:35–10:15 is an important passage about evangelism which illustrates most of the principles we noted in Part One. It records Jesus' evangelistic ministry in the cities and villages of Galilee, and shows that he taught in the synagogues, heralded the good news among the people, healed the sick, and was moved with tremendous compassion.

Matthew 9:35–
10:15 ☐

The needs of the people were so great that Jesus cried to God for more labourers. Then, in partial answer to his cry, he sent his twelve disciples in pairs to evangelise the needy people.

In 10:5–7, Jesus commanded the disciples *to herald the message*, provided them with the specific message that they were to proclaim, and directed them to a particular group of people. In 10:8, he told the disciples how *to demonstrate the message*. And, in 10:9–12, he instructed them how *to live the message* among the people whom they had been directed to reach.

It is vital that we recognise *whom* Jesus directed the disciples to reach. He sent them to evangelise (by proclaiming, demonstrating and living his good message) the *probata*, the *apololota*, 'the sheep, the lost' of Israel.

Luke 19:10 ☐

Matthew 10:28 ☐
          10:42 ☐

Mark 1:24 ☐
          9:22 ☐

Luke 9:25 ☐
          15:4 ☐

John 17:12 ☐
          3:16 ☐

Jesus used the same word in Luke 19:10 to describe his own evangelistic mission. He came to save *apololos*, 'the lost'.

Today, we usually think that the word 'lost' means missing or misplaced. The Greek word, however, is much stronger. It comes from the verb *apollumi* which means 'to destroy', or 'to ruin fully', or 'to spoil totally', or 'to lose completely'. We see this, for example, in Matthew 10:28, 42; Mark 1:24; 9:22; Luke 9:25; 15:4 and John 17:12.

Although some versions of the Bible translate *apollumi* as 'kill', it really means 'a loss of well-being' rather than 'a loss of being': it signifies devastation and ruin, not extinction and death.

Apollumi is occasionally translated into English as 'perish', as in John 3:16. This means that we can render this famous verse as, 'For God so loved the world that he gave his only begotten Son, that whoever believes in him should not be *lost* but have everlasting life.'

This shows that 'reaching the lost' is a thoroughly biblical expression; we must recognise, however, the grim seriousness of the state of 'lostness'. The lost have not wandered a few yards astray; they are utterly lost. They are so lost that they are perishing.

Nevertheless, although the lost are totally ruined and completely devastated, they still exist: the Son of Man came to save them, and he has sent us to reach them with the gospel of God's kingdom.

THE WORLD

John 3:16 is another important evangelistic verse. It contrasts everlasting life with 'ruin and lostness' rather than with 'death and extinction'; it teaches that the Father God is the great initiator of salvation; it shows that gracious love is the driving motive for his divine rescue mission; it establishes that God longs for nobody to be lost; and – most significantly – it reveals the *kosmos*, 'the world', as the object of God's love and the target of his mission.

Modern Christian thinking about evangelism usually focuses on individual men and women, but there is an inescapable 'whole world' dimension to the Bible. The Scriptures start, for example, with the creation of the world in Genesis 1, and climax with the new creation in Revelation 21.

Genesis 1 ☐
Revelation 21 ☐

In between, the Bible shows how sin spoils the whole creation, how God still loves his world, and how he acts to save it. Individualistic evangelism, which lacks a genuine 'world' dimension and ignores the eschatological hope of the 'new creation', is not biblical evangelism.

The New Testament uses *kosmos* about 170 times to highlight God's dealings with his world. *Kosmos* appears throughout the New Testament, but is most prominent in John and Paul's writings.

The Gospels

The Gospel writers use *kosmos* in several different ways to establish complementary principles. For example, 'the world' refers to:

Matthew 24:21 ☐
John 1:10 ☐
17:5 ☐
Matthew 4:8 ☐
Luke 12:30 ☐
John 6:14 ☐
Matthew 13:38 ☐
26:13 ☐
Mark 16:15 ☐

- *the material earth* – Matthew 24:21

- *the general created order* – John 1:10; 17:5

- *the order of existence into which men and women are born* – Matthew 4:8; Luke 12:30; John 6:14

- *the designated place for spreading the gospel* – Matthew 13:38; 26:13; Mark 16:15

John's Gospel focuses on God's relationship with the whole world. It shows, for example, that:

John 1:10 ☐
3:16–17 ☐
4:42 ☐
9:5 ☐
11:27 ☐

- *God made the world* – John 1:10

- *God loves the world* – John 3:16

- *God acts to save the world, not to condemn it* – John 3:17

- *Jesus is the Saviour of the world* – John 4:42

- *Jesus is the light of the world* – John 9:5

- *The Son of God comes into the world* – John 11:27

The Gospels also stress that the world is in conflict with God. They do not teach, however, that the world *is* itself inherently evil; instead, they show that it is *dominated by* evil. This is a crucial distinction, which is at the heart of the idea of 'lostness'.

The Gospel writers highlight this conflict by showing that the world:

- *is in spiritual darkness* – John 1:5; 8:12; 9:5

- *is antagonistic to Jesus* – John 7:7; 8:23

- *is dominated by evil* – John 12:31; 14:30; 16:11; 1 John 5:19

- *is passing* – 1 John 2:17

- *is ignorant of God* – John 1:10; 1 John 3:1

- *hates Christians* – 1 John 3:13

- *receives false prophets* – 1 John 4:1

- *listens to its own people* – 1 John 4:5

It should be clear that God would not love the world if it was inherently evil. But it is his world, he made it, and he is motivated by his infinite compassion to reach the lost world and rescue it from its domination by evil. This is why, in John 17:18, Jesus sent his disciples into the world in the same way that he was sent into the world. Like him, we are sent by God's love to reach the lost with the gospel.

Paul's epistles

In his epistles, the apostle Paul uses *kosmos* in a similar way. He refers to the God-created physical world in passages like Romans 1:20, 25; 1 Corinthians 4:9; Ephesians 3:9; Colossians 1:15–18; and, in Colossians 1:16, reveals that the whole world was made *for* Christ.

The vital principle that Jesus is 'the goal and purpose of the world' should transform the way that we think about the world, and should help us to understand more fully *why* there ought to be an environmental or 'new creation' dimension to our evangelism. Although we should focus on individual conversions we must never ignore the corporate and the cosmic elements of the gospel.

As in the Gospels, Paul also refers to the *kosmos* as:

- *the order of men and women* – 1 Timothy 6:7; 1 Corinthians 14:10; 1 Timothy 1:15; 2 Corinthians 1:12

- *in conflict with God* – Romans 3:6, 19; 1 Corinthians 1:20; 2:12; 3:19; 6:2; 11:32; Ephesians 2:12

- *passing* – 1 Corinthians 7:31

- *dominated by (not inherently) evil* – Ephesians 2:2; Philippians 2:15

Unlike the Gospels, Paul's epistles look back at the cross. He shows, in 2 Corinthians 5:19, this means that Christ has now reconciled 'the world' to God; and he stresses, in Colossians 2:20 and 2 Corinthians 10:3, that this should lead believers to live in the world in a new way and with a new attitude.

The 'cosmic', 'creation' or 'environmental' dimension of salvation is particularly clear in Romans 8:19–24, and we need to incorporate this difficult idea into our understanding of God's purposes for the world.

Some people seem to think that Romans 8 clashes with 2 Corinthians 5, but these chapters teach complementary truths which we need to hold together in parallel tension. 2 Corinthians 5 looks backwards towards the cross and rejoices in what God has done for individual men and women; whereas Romans 8 looks forward in hope to what God will do for the whole *kosmos* in the day of Revelation 21.

Most pentecostal and evangelical believers concentrate on the new creation *in* Christ of individual men and women. This is a right and biblical emphasis, but we should *also* look forward to the ultimate new creation *for* Christ of the whole world.

HUMANITY

Although our understanding of 'the lost' must embrace the entire cosmos, it is plain that humanity is by far the most important part of the created order.

We can begin to appreciate the full extent of humanity's 'lostness' only by considering Jesus' perfect humanity. Quite simply, he is God's revelation of what every person is meant to be.

We consider this in detail in *Knowing the Son*, but we should recognise here that Jesus provides the pattern by which all humanity is assessed. The Gospels present him as uniquely faultless: they describe his impact on other people, his compassion and concern for the needy,

1 Corinthians 7:31 ☐

Ephesians 2:2 ☐

Philippians 2:15 ☐

2 Corinthians 5:19 ☐

Colossians 2:20 ☐

2 Corinthians 10:3 ☐

Romans 8:19–24 ☐

Revelation 21 ☐

his revolutionary attitude to women and children, his kindness and generosity, his selflessness and sacrifice, his disregard for material possessions, his submission and obedience, and so on.

Compared to Jesus, every single man, woman and child is utterly 'lost' – is spoiled, ruined, devastated and perishing.

The Bible always considers people as whole beings who are infinitely valuable to God. Although the New Testament uses special words to refer to various aspects of the human being, it uses these words loosely and with considerable overlap. It does not consider people to be made of two, three or more distinct parts, but to be fully integrated beings.

The main words that the New Testament uses to describe different aspects of the human being are:

- **soul**, *psyche* – this generally refers to a person's whole life. Romans 11:3; 16:4; Philippians 2:30.

- **spirit**, *pneuma* – this describes the side of a person which, once awakened, is capable of responding to God. Before conversion, the spirit is 'dead' to God but 'alive' to the world, the flesh and the devil. The spirit is 'revived' at conversion by the Holy Spirit so that we can respond to God and live in fellowship with him. The revived spirit can be defiled or consecrated, but it is meant to be devoted to God and dominated by him. Romans 8:16; 1 Corinthians 7:34; 16:18; 2 Corinthians 2:13; 7:1, 13.

- **flesh**, *sarx* – this usually represents a person in their earthly origin, natural weakness and alienation from God. It is closely allied to sin, and is often the cause of sinful activity. Romans 1:3; 3:20; 7; 1 Corinthians 1:29; 2 Corinthians 10:3; Galatians 1:16; 5:16–19.

- **body**, *soma* – this refers to a person's literal physical structure. It is supposed to be a temple for the Holy Spirit, and is not meant to be used for immoral activity. Although the body is mortal, God can give it life; and it is due for resurrection and redemption. Romans 8:10–11, 23; 1 Corinthians 6:13, 18–20; Philippians 3:21.

- **heart**, *kardia* – this normally points to the whole inner person. It can stand for the centre of a person's life, the will, the emotions, or the motivational centre of a person. Psalms 9:1; 16:9; 112:7; 119:10; Proverbs 2:2; 3:5; 23:26; Romans 10:10; 1 Corinthians 4:5; 7:37; 2 Corinthians 2:4; 3:3; 4:6; 7:2; Ephesians 1:17–18; Galatians 4:6; Colossians 3:16.

- **mind**, *nous* – this describes a person's total mental activities: intellect, thinking and understanding. Its condition or morality depends on whether it is dominated by God, blinded by Satan, or controlled by the 'flesh'. It functions properly only when it has been renewed and conforms to God's mind. Romans 1:28; 7:13–25; 12:2; 1 Corinthians 2:16; 2 Corinthians 4:4–6.

- **conscience**, *syneidesis* – this enables people to be aware of themselves as rational, moral beings; and it shows them what is 'right', independent of their own standards. It is the capacity to determine what is right, and does not involve the exercise of the will. When the conscience is persistently disobeyed, it becomes defiled and hardened. Romans 2:15; 9:1; 1 Corinthians 8:7; 10:25; 2 Corinthians 1:12; 1 Timothy 4:2.

HUMANITY AND SIN

Every man, woman and child was meant to be like the human Jesus. Each integrated being – incorporating an overlapping soul, spirit, flesh, body, heart, mind and conscience – was made to be directed by God and to live in perpetual, perfect fellowship with him.

But none are. All humanity is lost or perishing; it has been 'ruined', 'spoilt', 'devastated' by sin. Quite simply, the lost are perishing because of sin. We examine this more fully in *Salvation by Grace*, but we need to realise here the full extent of sin's impact on humanity.

The Bible teaches that:

- *sin is universal* – Romans 1–3; 5:12

- *sin is internal attitudes and external actions* – Romans 1:29–31; 13:13; 1 Corinthians 5:10–13; 6:9–10; 2 Corinthians 12:20–21; Galatians 5:19–21; Ephesians 4:31; 5:3–5; Colossians 3:5–8; 1 Timothy 1:9–10; 2 Timothy 3:2–3; Titus 3:3

- *sin is enslavement to Satan* – 1 John 3:8–10

- *sin is a slave-master* – Romans 6:16–17

- *sin is rebellion against God* – Luke 15:11–32

John 7:7 ☐
         9:41 ☐

Romans 5:10 ☐

1 John 2:16 ☐

John 5:24 ☐
         16:9 ☐
         1:4–9 ☐
         8:12 ☐

1 John 2:8–9 ☐

Romans 6:19 ☐

2 Corinthians
         6:14 ☐

1 John 3:4 ☐

Matthew 6:12 ☐

Colossians 2:14 ☐

Romans 1:18, 25 ☐

Ephesians 4:25 ☐

2 Thessalonians
         2:11–12 ☐

1 Timothy 6:5 ☐

Romans 2:23 ☐

John 3:36 ☐

Romans 11:30 ☐

Ephesians 2:2 ☐

Matthew 12:36 ☐

Luke 12:47–48 ☐

Matthew
         11:20–24 ☐

Romans 6:21–23 ☐
         7:13 ☐

- *sin is alienation from God* – John 7:7; 9:41; Romans 5:10; 1 John 2:16

- *sin is unbelief* – John 5:24; 16:9

- *sin is blindness and darkness* – John 1:4–9; 8:12; 1 John 2:8–9

- *sin is lawlessness* – Romans 6:19; 2 Corinthians 6:14; 1 John 3:4

- *sin is debt* – Matthew 6:12; Colossians 2:14

- *sin is falsehood* – Romans 1:18, 25; Ephesians 4:25; 2 Thessalonians 2:11–12; 1 Timothy 6:5

- *sin is deviation* – Romans 2:23

- *sin is disobedience* – John 3:36; Romans 11:30; Ephesians 2:2

- *sin merits condemnation by God* – Matthew 12:36; Luke 12:47–48; Matthew 11:20–24

- *sin leads to death* – Romans 6:21–23; 7:13

The Bible makes it clear that nobody – except Jesus – is as they ought to be: they are all 'lost' or 'perishing'. Different parts of the Scriptures describe this in slightly different ways, but the overall picture is clear.

Humanity has rebelled against God; it has disobeyed God's laws; it has allowed itself to come into a bondage to sin from which it cannot escape by its own efforts. As a result, humanity is blind to its own potential and ignorant of God. This is expressed by humanity's refusal to believe in Christ – who alone can rescue it from sin, reconcile it with God and restore it to its rightful state.

The Bible also makes it plain that human sin deserves divine punishment. We consider this more fully in *Salvation by Grace*, but we must appreciate here that the condemnation of sin by a righteous God is a basic assumption of salvation. We cannot fully understand Jesus' evangelistic mission without grasping this important truth.

In fact, all the facets of sin that we have noted are basic to Christ's gospel mission. For example, if sin is enslavement, Jesus brings deliverance; if it is falsehood, he brings truth; if it is debt, he brings forgiveness; if it is alienation, he brings reconciliation; if it is disobedience, he shows the way of obedience; if it is deviation, he sets the example of righteousness; if it merits condemnation, he has borne the punishment; and so on.

KNOWING THE LOST

If we are to reach the lost with the gospel, we need to know not only their true spiritual condition, we also need to know them and their concerns. And if the *ptochos* are to be the focus of our evangelistic mission, we need to know their particular afflictions and hurts.

We have seen that Jesus was anointed with the Spirit to evangelise those who are afflicted by sin, by Satan and by society.

Sin hurts people; and the consequences of sin include emotional pain, broken relationships and wounded lives. All people are afflicted by sin – they are blinded, oppressed and held captive by sin.

It is the same with Satan. As we see in *Ministry in the Spirit*, he is the deceiver and destroyer of humanity; he is an evil defamer and a despotic ruler. All people are held captive by Satan as 'prisoners-of-war' and he feeds on their fear and distress.

But we must also recognise that society inflicts deep hurt. People are financially, politically and emotionally afflicted because of the way that society works. It oppresses and isolates people; it blinds them to justice and truth; it devalues and depersonalises them. Society breaks their hearts, steals their hope, strips them of their humanity and holds them captive to its false values.

When we think about people and modern society, we can see that they are afflicted by, for example:

- *fear of violence and crime*

- *health and job worries*

- *family breakdown*

- *materialism*

- *debt*

- *social isolation, insignificance and loneliness*

- *superstitions*

- *self-pity, self-hatred and guilt*

- *immoral and amoral ideas*

Luke 4:18 ☐

Some of this is not new, for the ordinary people of Jesus' day were afflicted by their society – by their Roman conquerors, the Jewish religious authorities, double and corrupt taxation, disease and food shortages, a sense of powerlessness and insignificance, and all the pressures of their short lives.

The Gospels show that Jesus knew them and knew their hurts. He lived among the *ptochos* and shared their afflictions because he loved them with the infinite love of God. He overlooked their lack of status and education, appreciated their true eternal worth, and upset the social conventions of his day by treating them as the equals of the educated, powerful elite.

Obviously, the words of Luke 4:18 do have a spiritual application: Jesus did come for the spiritually lost, the spiritually imprisoned, the spiritually blind, the spiritually poor, and so on.

But the Gospels suggest that he also meant these words literally, for the religious leaders of his day were continually affronted by the way that Jesus welcomed, mixed with, and helped, beggars, lepers, tax-collectors, women with 'certain reputations', unclean sinners, the terminally ill, and so on.

This implies that we should be as focused as Jesus on reaching the lost people who inhabit the fringes of modern life – as well as more prosperous lost people and ordinary lost men and women outside the church. And, like Jesus, our action should not be patronising, it should be the genuine affection of God.

If we share Christ's anointing, we surely also share the purpose of his anointing. He sends us deep into the *kosmos* to reach with his compassion all those are afflicted and hurting – and this includes the alienated young, the isolated elderly, the homeless, the unemployed, immigrant groups, ethnic minorities, as well as the humble poor.

PART THREE

motives for evangelism

Evangelism is not easy. Many believers try to reach the lost with the good news of Jesus, but give up when they become discouraged. And many churches have not persisted with their primary task of evangelism because they have experienced real disappointment.

Even though there are vast numbers of courses and conferences on evangelism, and all sorts of schemes and strategies, most believers are not actively seeking to reach the lost with the gospel – and, therefore, the overwhelming majority of lost people are not being reached.

The problem is simple. It is motivation. It is easier to devise a strategy than to motivate a disappointed disciple, and more straight-forward to arrange a conference than to activate a discouraged Christian.

Discouragement

Even Jesus was not immune to discouragement and disappointment. John 6 reports how vast crowds came to hear him: they were drawn by the wonderful miracles that they had witnessed, and Jesus taught

John 6 ☐

them that he was the real bread of life and that they needed to eat his flesh to have real life.

Jesus made exclusive, authoritative, attractive claims – yet the people 'murmured against him'. Verses 41, 52, 60–61 and 66 describe how Jesus was misunderstood, misrepresented and rejected. Even some of his disciples turned their backs on him and walked away. It is almost possible to feel Jesus' acute disappointment in verse 67.

2 Corinthians 4 □

It was the same for the apostle Paul. In 2 Corinthians 4, he describes the pressures that he faced to stop evangelising. Twice he affirms that he refused to lose heart – which seems to suggest that this was a temptation which he knew rather well.

Blindness

2 Corinthians 4:2–6 describes the spiritual blindness of the people whom Paul was trying to reach. They were not interested in the good news that he brought and could not see the relevance of the gospel he was proclaiming.

Verse 3 refers to the *apollumenois* – to the 'lost' or the 'perishing' – and shows that their minds have been blinded to the gospel. This explains why evangelism is so hard: blindness is the main reason for the lost's indifference – and, therefore, for our discouragement.

In verse 6, Paul explains how he kept evangelising in the face of this discouraging apathy. He knew that God could cause light to shine from darkness. He knew that he had been blind, and that God had shone the light of Jesus into his heart. Paul knew that God could do for anyone what God had done for him; so he refused to lose heart.

Tiredness

2 Corinthians 11:22–33 □

In 2 Corinthians 4:7–15, Paul describes the physical and mental exhaustion which also tempted him to lose heart – and he adds to this in 11:22–33.

He knew what it meant to be afflicted, perplexed, persecuted, struck down and constantly facing death: it was all intensely wearying. Paul knew that the discouraging tiredness and pain would cease if he stopped evangelising. But he refused to lose heart.

In verses 16–18, Paul explains how he managed to keep evangelising when he was mentally and physically exhausted. He knew that his present physical condition was preparing him for a 'far more exceeding and eternal weight of glory'.

Paul had an eternal and spiritual perspective. He knew that his tiredness was merely a temporary condition, and that what was before him in heaven infinitely outweighed the temporary discomfort of his present difficulties. And he knew that, although his physical body really was slowly perishing, his inner spiritual man was being renewed every day – and this was far more important.

In 2 Corinthians 5:9–21, Paul moves on to describe five factors which motivated his evangelism. As these are set against this 2 Corinthians 4 backdrop of disappointment and discouragement, we can be sure that the factors are not just theories: they are the practical motives which prompted Paul to overcome his discouragement and disappointment, and to keep on reaching the lost with the good news about Jesus.

2 Corinthians 5:9–21 ☐

THE JUDGEMENT OF CHRIST

2 Corinthians 5:10–11 shows that 'the terror of the Lord', the truth of Christ's judgement, was a primary motive for Paul's evangelistic activity. He knew that he would appear before Christ's throne to be judged – this is underlined in 1 Corinthians 3:5–15.

1 Corinthians 3:5–15 ☐

Our judgement

Many of Jesus' parables teach that we will have to account for the gifts and opportunities which God has given us. We will have to explain to Christ how we have used our time, money, gifts and energy in the work of the gospel.

We may be able to deceive others, and justify our inactivity to ourselves, but 1 Corinthians 4:1–5 shows that Christ will expose the secret purposes of our heart. When we have a real concept of the Judgement Day, and of the rewards which will flow to the faithful

1 Corinthians 4:1–5 ☐

1 Corinthians
    3:15 ☐

– and the corresponding loss and disappointment which will flow to the unfaithful – we will do all that we can to reach the lost with the gospel. We see this in 1 Corinthians 3:15.

Their judgement

The lost will themselves also be judged by Christ on that great and terrible Day. Their blind eyes will be opened and they will see themselves as they really are.

Many of the lost seem to be good and decent people; they are concerned for others, they work hard for a fairer society, they lead contented, peaceable lives – and their spiritual lostness is not immediately obvious. But Christ will divide people into only two categories when he judges the world – the sheep and the goats, the righteous and the unrighteous, the saved and the lost, and so on.

Jesus gives the clearest, strongest and most detailed biblical teaching about the last judgement. He announces the good news of salvation *and* he warns the lost about judgement and calls them to repentance.

This means that our awareness of judgement, our grasp of heaven and hell, should compel us to reach compassionately to the lost with both holy warnings *and* gospel forgiveness.

When we grasp something of Paul's right-and-healthy 'terror of the Lord', we will be effected in two positive ways:

- *we will be urgent in our evangelism* – we will use every means and opportunity to herald the message because we want to earn our 'well-done' and to turn people away from destruction.

2 Corinthians
    4:2 ☐
    5:11 ☐
    6:3 ☐

1 Thessalonians
    1:5 ☐

- *we will live consistently with our message* – 2 Corinthians 4:2; 5:11; 6:3 and 1 Thessalonians 1:5 reveal Paul's confidence in his personal integrity. The more we contemplate Christ's judgement, the more we will live in alignment with the gospel.

Throughout history, a clear understanding of the judgement of Christ has been one of the church's greatest motivating forces to evangelism.

Of course, this can be corrupted into a 'hell-fire' type of preaching which lacks compassion and is absent from the New Testament; but those congregations which ignore the truth of Christ's judgement usually lack evangelistic urgency.

THE LOVE OF CHRIST

2 Corinthians 5:14 reveals that 'the love of Christ' was another powerful motive which drove Paul to keep evangelising – even when he faced disappointments and discouragements, apathy and exhaustion.

In this verse, Paul uses the Greek verb *sunecho* which is often translated as 'constrain' or 'control'. It means being 'pressed' or 'seized', and is used to describe being 'controlled' by a disease, 'seized' by a person, 'gripped' by fear, and 'pressing' fingers into ears – for example, Matthew 4:24; Luke 4:38; 8:37, 45; 12:50; 19:43; 22:63; Acts 7:57; 28:8.

Some translations suggest that Jesus was 'distressed' in Luke 12:50, but the word is *sunecho*. This means that Jesus was gripped by a powerful motivating force which was urging him towards the cross. It is the same in 2 Corinthians 5:14: Paul was 'pressed', 'gripped' or 'controlled' by God's love: this is the holy force which motivated him to overcome his personal discouragements and keep evangelising.

In 2 Corinthians 5:14, Paul writes about God's love in the context of *Calvary*. Verse 15 shows that the cross meant Paul could no longer live for himself. He had been bought with a price and therefore had to live for the sake of the Son who had loved him so much.

In Romans 5:5, Paul writes about God's love in the context of *Pentecost*. And whenever the New Testament describes disciples being filled with the Spirit, it shows that evangelism soon follows – we see this, for example, in Acts 2:4–11; 4:31–34 and 9:17–22.

We can say that the love of God was revealed to the disciples at Calvary and was poured into them at Pentecost, and that it was this compassionate divine love which motivated them to evangelise.

Too many modern believers evangelise out of a sense of duty rather than out of a life which is gripped and moved by God's love. 1 Thessalonians 2:8 shows that we are called not only to 'give them the gospel', we are also called to give them our lives.

If we are not filled with God's love, we are unlikely to be motivated to evangelise, for the poverty of our spiritual lives will mean that we have little to say. But a fresh experience of God's love will soon 'constrain' us to start spreading the good news about Jesus.

2 Corinthians
5:14 ☐

Matthew 4:24 ☐
Luke 4:38 ☐
8:37 ☐
8:45 ☐
12:50 ☐
19:43 ☐
22:63 ☐
Acts 7:57 ☐
28:8 ☐

Romans 5:5 ☐
Acts 2:4–11 ☐
4:31–34 ☐
9:17–22 ☐

1 Thessalonians
2:8 ☐

THE POWER OF CHRIST

2 Corinthians 5:15–17 ☐

2 Corinthians 5:17 points graphically to the great power of Christ. Translated literally, it reads like a newspaper headline, 'If anyone is in Christ – new creation'. This is the marvellous motivation of the gospel.

The power of Christ is the only force in the cosmos which can change human nature. Jesus has much to say about our behaviour and attitudes, but he always begins by offering us a new heart and a new spirit.

Once we grasp the great power of Christ, our attitude towards people is transformed. We see this in 2 Corinthians 5:16. Instead of viewing people as they are, we see their potential in Christ. This is the view that Ananias had in Acts 9:17, when he greeted the man who had come to Damascus to arrest him as, '*Brother* Saul'.

Acts 9:17 ☐

Paul knew from personal experience that a fanatical opponent of the followers of Christ had become a new creation. He knew therefore, that God could do it for 'anyone' – and this motivated his mission.

Even though Paul was a great debater, he knew that people had to be 'in Christ' to be a new creation. Evangelism does not consist of convincing people that we are right, it consists of introducing them to Jesus.

This does not mean that we do not answer people's questions, and do not deal with the deep issues which concern them. Instead, it means we recognise that, *on their own*, words and argument are not enough. We see this in 1 Corinthians 2:4–5.

1 Corinthians 2:4–5 ☐

Like Paul, we often need to persuade people by answering their objections and demonstrating the reasonableness of our faith. But our primary concern must always be to lead people into Christ, and not to win an argument or score a debating point.

When evangelism gets hard, and we are faced with difficult people who are opposed to the gospel, the knowledge that nothing is too hard for God will keep us going.

And when we know for certain that absolutely anyone can be transformed by the power of Christ, we will be motivated to keep on reaching out to the 'lostest' of the lost without losing heart.

THE MINISTRY OF CHRIST

2 Corinthians 5:18 reveals another important motive for reaching the lost. We have been given Christ's ministry of reconciliation.

2 Corinthians 5:18 □

One of the great themes which runs through this *School of Ministry in the Word and the Spirit* is the 2 Corinthians 6:1 truth that we do not have our own ministry, we have a share in Christ's ministry. We focus on this principle in *Glory in the Church* and *Ministry in the Spirit*.

2 Corinthians 6:1 □

If we had our own ministry of evangelism, it would be for us to decide how much time and energy we should commit to the ministry. But, as it is Christ's ministry, we must follow his example and obey him in everything.

2 Corinthians 5:18 states that we have been entrusted with a share in Christ's ministry of *reconciliation*. When evangelicals and pentecostals think about the cross, they often stress *redemption, justification* and *forgiveness*. These are important biblical aspects of Christ's saving work on the cross, but their common purpose is *reconciliation*.

We have been 'redeemed' with a price so that we can be reconciled; God has declared us 'justified' because of Christ's death so that we can be reconciled with him; he has 'forgiven' us on the basis of Christ's blood so that we can be reconciled with him; and so on. As we see in *Salvation by Grace*, reconciliation is not just another way of looking at Christ's death, it is the great purpose behind every way of looking at his death.

It should be obvious that the ideas of 'reconciliation' and 'lostness' go together. The greatest need of the lost is to be found – to be brought back to where they should be, to be restored to the relationship for which they were made, and so on. This is why all Jesus' parables about the cross focus on lostness and reconciliation.

The essence of reconciliation is bringing together two estranged parties. But, before this can take place, the cause of the estrangement must be dealt with. As mediator, Jesus brought humanity and God together by taking upon himself the cause of the separation – sin.

In *Knowing the Father*, we establish that Jesus was an 'inclusive mediator' not an 'exclusive mediator'. He went for us where we could not go so that we can follow after him and do what we could not do.

And, having accomplished this *kosmos* reconciliation in Christ, God has now entrusted us with this gracious ministry of reconciliation.

Reconciliation

Christ's ministry of reconciliation is central to evangelism. We announce, demonstrate and live the good news so that men and women will be reconciled with God through Christ.

Jesus was both the perfect example of reconciliation and the ultimate reconciler. Because he was both fully God *and* fully human, he incarnated reconciliation. And because he lived in an intimate relationship with God *and* with people, he could effect reconciliation.

This means that we must be both close to God *and* close to people to minister reconciliation effectively.

Evangelism fails when we are not close to God. Without prayer, total dependence on the Spirit, and a knowledge of God's will and Word, we will fall back on human strategies and traditions. Lifeless, loveless, legalistic evangelism does not draw the lost to God – it drives them even further away. Whereas evangelism which overflows from a living, loving relationship with God does attract the lost to God. Slick words are never a substitute for sincere compassion.

But evangelism also fails when we are not close to people. Jesus has sent us into the world to be the salt of the world. Yet many believers are so enveloped in church-based activities that they have virtually no contact with the world. As a result, their evangelism can seem artificial and contrived, rather than the natural outcome of genuine friendship.

THE DEATH OF CHRIST

2 Corinthians
5:18–21 ☐

Hebrews 12:3 ☐

2 Corinthians 5:18–21 shows that the cross itself is the final compelling motive for biblical evangelism; this is underlined by Hebrews 12:3.

In verse 21, it is if Paul is trying to summarise all the motives which enabled him to overcome discouragement and disappointment. Paul realised that the sinless Jesus had become sin for him so that he could become the righteousness of God in Christ – and it was the wonder of this which drove him on to reach the lost with this good news.

Sometimes we become complacent about Calvary. The words and ideas are so familiar that we do not appreciate the enormity of the divine sacrifice. Verse 21 shows that Paul was motivated to evangelise by his stark awareness that, at Calvary, God had poured all the filth and pain of human sin onto perfect Jesus – to the ghastly extent that Christ actually became sin.

Paul writes about reconciliation in Colossians 1:19–22, and stresses that God made peace with us through the blood of the cross. This proves that evangelism was not easy for Jesus, for the ministry of reconciliation literally cost him his life. In order to reconcile the world, Jesus had to appropriate human sin and experience human 'lostness' for himself.

Colossians
1:19–22 ☐

This, then, is the ministry that we are called to share with Christ as fellow workers. It involves sacrifice; it embraces the holiness of God and the filth of the world, and it draws them together in Christ. This is the wonderful way that God has chosen to reveal himself to his lost world, and we have a vital part in it. Like Paul, we must not lose heart.

PART FOUR

the message of evangelism

We have seen that the herald's proclamation of the king's message is a key feature of biblical evangelism. We may not reach the lost only by preaching or witnessing to them, nevertheless, a verbal announcement of the good news must accompany a visual demonstration of the gospel in signs, wonders and Christ-like living.

GOD'S MESSAGE

In Part One, we noted that the gospel is both good news *from* the triune God and good news *about* the triune God. It is *his* message; it is the king's good news.

In *Living Faith* and *Listening to God*, we establish that every word, every revelation, from God is essentially a self-revelation. We see this in the Hebrew word *dabar*, but we see it most clearly in Jesus – who is

God's Personal Word. This underlines the fact that the gospel is essentially a self revelation of God's gracious nature – it is his good news about himself.

The apostle Paul stresses this in 1 Corinthians 2:1: he did not bring human wisdom; rather, he brought the testimony of God. We have seen that Paul considered himself a herald, and this meant that he delivered his master's message without adding, altering or omitting anything.

It was the same with Jesus. John 12:49–50 shows how Jesus restricted himself to speaking what the Father had commanded him to say. The gospel that he proclaimed was the gospel that the Father had given him to proclaim: Jesus added, altered and omitted nothing.

It is almost impossible to over-emphasise this truth. The message we proclaim is not ours to adjust as we fancy: it is God's personal message to the lost and must be passed on as such.

Although, like Jesus with the Samaritan woman, we need to explain the message in relevant terms which communicate with the lost, we must not alter the kernel of the gospel to make it more 'acceptable'.

God as Creator

In Genesis, the Bible introduces God as *Creator*, and throughout both Testaments he is continually revealed as the only Maker of heaven and earth, and of all things on the earth.

We see this, for example, in Genesis 1:1; Deuteronomy 4:32; Psalm 89:12; 148:5; Ecclesiastes 12:1; Isaiah 40:28; 42:5; 43:15; 45:8; 65:17; Ezekiel 28:13–15; Amos 4:13; Malachi 2:10; Mark 13:19; Ephesians 3:9; Colossians 1:16; 1 Timothy 4:3; 1 Peter 4:19; Revelation 4:11.

Throughout the twentieth century, many believers and churches did not reveal God as Creator because they thought that this was an unacceptable truth in a scientific age. We can say, however, that God's unique paternal authority rests on his unique creatorship, and that Jesus' unquestioned lordship of the universe is rooted in the fact that creation was made by-and-for him. If we are ignore the foundation, our conclusion will always appear to be unreasonable.

Whenever believers choose not to announce the news of God's creatorship, they are likely to fall into two serious errors.

- *They neglect the 'kosmos' side of the gospel and overlook the hope of the 'new creation'.*

- *They evangelise in a way which suggests that men and women are central to the universe.*

In evangelism, if we do not proclaim God as Creator and Lord, we are almost bound to focus on human needs rather than the divine demand to bend the knee to Jesus. We must remember that the heart of the gospel is not the human-centred news that 'Jesus will meet *your* needs', and it is not helping *people* to decide whether or not Jesus is real. God is not in our dock. We are in his dock.

We must remember that Jesus' gospel is the news that the kingdom, the personal rule of God, has come. The rightful ruler now commands us to end our rebellion, to accept the reconciliation which he has made, and to acknowledge his rule in every area of our lives. God can make these claims because he created us – we belong to him. Human-centred evangelism is short-sighted, unscriptural, and sure to fail.

When we accept that God is Creator (and therefore Lord) we start to realise that every aspect of life matters to him. If he is Creator, he is inevitably concerned with the whole of his creation – with his entire *kosmos*. He is concerned with working conditions, fair trade, pollution, the state of the cities, the gap between rich and poor, justice, war, family breakdown, the weapons trade, abortion, euthanasia, genetic experimentation, international debt, deforestation, and so on.

Whether we realise it or not, everybody has to deal with five sets of problems:

- *personal problems*

- *family problems*

- *community problems*

- *national problems*

- *global problems*

All these sets of problems interact with each other, but God the Creator is concerned with all five, and has acted in salvation to resolve all five and to reconcile his whole world with himself.

Too often, modern believers preach a gospel which suggests that God is concerned only with personal problems, and that God does not have any message – let alone gospel 'good news' – about global, national and community problems. But God is the Creator, and this aspect of his self-revelation must be part of our evangelistic proclamation.

God as Redeemer

Both testaments of the Bible also consistently present God as *Redeemer*. We see this, for example, in Deuteronomy 15:15; 21:8; 24:18; 2 Samuel 7:23; 1 Chronicles 17:21; Nehemiah 1:10; Job 19:25; Psalm 19:14; 31:5; 49:15; 72:14; 74:2; 77:15; 78:35; 103:4; Proverbs 23:11; Isaiah 43:14; 44:22–24; 47:4; 52:9; 63:16; Jeremiah 15:21; 50:34; Lamentations 3:58; Micah 4:10; Zechariah 10:8; Luke 1:68; Galatians 3:13; 4:5 and Revelation 5:9.

Today, in their evangelism, too many believers proclaim God exclusively as Redeemer. But biblical evangelism always proclaims the double-bladed revelation of God as Creator *and* Redeemer. We see this particularly clearly in Acts 17:22–34. In fact, it is essentially because God is the Creator that he acts as the Redeemer to reconcile *his* world.

In the Old Testament, 'to redeem' means to free or release someone by paying a debt or avenging a wrong. In those days, only a *close relative* could redeem another person; so, in Ruth 4:1–11, Boaz redeemed his relation Ruth by buying back the land and property of Elimelech.

God, therefore, was recognised as Israel's Redeemer because he acted to free *his children* from their corporate slavery to other nations. This is why Isaiah 63:16 describes God as 'our Father, our Redeemer'.

In the New Testament, Paul borrowed the idea of 'redemption' from contemporary life. In those days, 'redemption' referred to the price which was paid to release a slave from bondage and to ransom a prisoner-of-war, and it was used by the early church as a picture of Christ's work in releasing believers from the captivity of sin and the slavery of the Law.

The cross of Jesus Christ is central to the biblical revelation of God as Redeemer, for it was there, by his shed blood, that Christ accomplished both individual salvation and *kosmos* reconciliation. Passages like 1 Corinthians 1:18–23 and 15:1–14 show that 'Christ crucified; Christ resurrected' is at the heart of the good news.

A BIBLICAL MESSAGE

In every age, on every continent, throughout all traditions, the cross has been continually recognised as the universal symbol of the Christian faith. Quite simply, the cross is central to the whole Bible and to the full gospel message.

The cross in the Old Testament

Right from Genesis 3:15, the Old Testament prepares the way for the cross. Story after story, Psalm after Psalm, prophecy after prophecy, point forward to the cross.

Genesis 3:15 ☐

For example, the story of Abraham and Isaac on Mount Moriah, in Genesis 22, describes Isaac's total trust in his father and his ready submission – however costly – to everything that Abraham said and did. The phrase in 22:6, 'the two of them set out together' anticipates Jesus' complete trust in his Father, and his perfect submission – even to death on a cross.

Genesis 22 ☐

The story of Joseph and his brothers foreshadows many aspects of Jesus' death and resurrection. Joseph makes true claims about himself which arouse jealousy and hatred; he is especially loved by his father; he is rejected by his brothers, but God raises him to an exalted position; he lays up vast stores of grain so that he can feed all those who come to him when their human resources have been exhausted, and so on.

Genesis 37–47 ☐

All this points to Jesus' rejection, and his ability and willingness – through death and resurrection – to give life and satisfaction to all those who are humble enough to come to him for sustenance.

The story of Israel's deliverance from slavery in Egypt foreshadows a different aspect of the cross. When, after many warning plagues, Pharaoh still refused to release God's people, God told Moses and Aaron that each Israelite household should sacrifice a perfect lamb or goat and sprinkle some of the blood on the doorposts of their homes. That night, God killed the firstborn of every family and farm animal in Egypt – but he 'passed over' the households whose homes were marked with blood.

Exodus 11–12 ☐

Today, the judgement of God and the righteous sentence of death hang over every household in the world, but the perfect lamb has been sacrificed at Calvary, and those who trust in his blood will be spared when the great and terrible day of judgement finally comes.

The heroic story of David and Goliath, in 1 Samuel 17, reveals a further aspect of the cross. Another enemy, more deadly than Goliath, and at the head of an army more powerful and numerous than the Philistines, threatened the people of God. Another despised and unrecognised descendant of Jesse – Jesus of Bethlehem – achieved a final and total victory over the adversary and his hosts, completely breaking his power for those who believe.

And, just as David went triumphantly back to Jerusalem after the battle, leaving the Israelites to press home his victory over the Philistines, so Jesus returned to heaven, leaving his foot-soldiers to press home by faith his victory over a defeated foe.

Well-known Old Testament passages like Psalm 22 and Isaiah 53 point to Jesus' sufferings on the cross with stunning accuracy, but the shadow of the cross falls across all thirty nine books, and every aspect of the good news can be glimpsed in advance.

In fact, the cross is so plain in the Old Testament that Jesus rebuked Cleopas and his companion, in Luke 24:13–27, because they had not understood what the prophets had written. Jesus then took them through the Old Testament scriptures to show them how it had been revealed that the Messiah would suffer the cross and enter his glory.

The cross in the New Testament

The cross dominates the New Testament. For example, over a third of the Gospels is taken up with Christ's sufferings; John the Baptist's first comment about Jesus pointed to his death; Moses and Elijah spoke about Jesus' coming death at the transfiguration; and, as soon as the disciples had recognised him as the Son of God, Jesus taught them about his coming death and resurrection. We see this in John 1:29; Luke 9:30–31 and Matthew 16:21–23.

In his epistles, Paul keeps on returning to the cross, and Galatians 6:14 epitomises his writing and preaching. Today, many believers glory in Jesus' miracles, while others glory in his teaching or holy example. Paul, however, knew that the cross was central – because there the Father made the Son sin for us so that we could be reconciled with God: this, and nothing else, is the essence of the gospel.

The book of Hebrews is pre-occupied with the achievements of the cross, and considers Christ's death in the light of the Old Testament as the fulfilment of the sacrificial system. It stresses that we can confidently enter God's holy presence only because Christ has offered himself as the once-and-for-all single sacrifice for sin. We see this, for example, in Hebrews 9:26; 10:12, 19.

Peter's epistles provide some of the simplest scriptural teaching about the cross in 1 Peter 3:18; and John's epistles emphasise that the blood is the basis of reconciliation and fellowship in 1 John 1:7.

Even the book of Revelation, with its focus on the last days, is centred on the lamb who was slain; and it reveals that all heavenly worship revels in the glories of the cross. We see this in Revelation 5.

Hebrews 9:26 ☐
10:12 ☐
10:19 ☐
1 Peter 3:18 ☐
1 John 1:7 ☐
Revelation 5 ☐

A HISTORICAL MESSAGE

This simple biblical overview should remind us that the cross is central to the Scriptures and, therefore, should be central in our evangelism.

On its own, however, the recital of Scriptural principles is often inadequate. In this sceptical age, people often dismiss the story of Jesus as a fable or try to interpret it as a myth. This means that we must be able to anchor our gospel message in actual historical events.

The gospel is not only a subjective message about love, joy and peace, it is also an objective message which is rooted in true, well-documented historical events. We need to grasp just how strong and credible are the facts of the Gospels, and to pass this message on.

Documentary evidence

Obviously no historical account of anything can be absolutely 'proved' in every detail. But we can answer intelligent questions about when the Gospels were written, whether they refers to facts known from other sources, whether the copies we possess reflect what was originally written, and whether the events they record are corroborated by independent records.

As far as the Gospels are concerned, we have:

- *some fragments of the Greek New Testament which are dated to within twenty years of Jesus' death*

- *most of the New Testament in an early third century Greek text, and numerous fragments from the third century*

- *ever-increasing numbers of fairly complete Greek texts of the New Testament from the fourth century*

- *several complete fourth century manuscripts in five different languages which were translated from the original Greek in the second to fourth century*

- *over 20,000 quotes from the New Testament in other writings in the first to third centuries*

In short, the textual evidence for the wording of the modern New Testament is incomparably better and greater than any other ancient work. There can be no reasoned argument about this.

Archaeological evidence

Modern archaeology has verified most of the incidental details in the New Testament. This shows that the writers were accurate observers, and also helps to establish when the books were written.

For example, the Gospel of Luke refers correctly to fifteen different titles for different Roman governors. This demonstrates its general reliability and proves that it could not have been written after the time of the events it records.

In the nineteenth century, most scholars thought that the bulk of the New Testament was not written in the first century. But independent twentieth century archaeology has forced modern scholars to keep on pushing back the date when the New Testament was written.

The historical, topographical and archaeological accuracy of the Gospels means that most experts now accept that most of the New Testament books were written between AD 45–70.

This is rather like a man in his sixties writing today about the main events of his thirties: nobody would question his ability to write accurately about the events he saw first-hand. This means that the

Gospels provide the earliest, best, and most accurate record of Jesus. There is no archaeological evidence which discredits them.

Independent evidence

Because the early church met in homes and rejected statues, archaeologists are not likely to find early monuments which mention Christ. They have, however, discovered:

- *an AD 49 inscription in Galilee which threatens the death penalty for anyone who removes a body from a tomb*

- *some AD 50 tombs in Jerusalem which are engraved with 'Jesus help' and 'Jesus let him arise'*

- *tombs containing Christian symbols and inscriptions which have been dated to AD 79 in Pompeii and AD 95 in Rome*

It is also unlikely that non-Christian sources would record Jesus' miracles and resurrection, but Roman and Jewish writings from AD 50–150, do mention Jesus and his followers. They report that:

- *Jesus lived in Judaea*

- *he kept and taught high moral standards*

- *people ascribed miracles to him and his followers*

- *Jesus' followers regarded him as a Messiah or divine figure*

- *he was put to death under Pilate*

- *he was crucified*

- *in AD 64, his followers were falsely blamed by Nero for a great fire in Rome and were persecuted*

For example, the Roman historian Tacitus (who died in AD 120) wrote that Emperor Nero:

'inflicted the most cruel tortures on a group of people detested for their abominations and popularly known as "Christians". They got their name from Christ, who was executed by sentence of the procurator Pontius Pilate in the reign of Tiberius. This checked the pernicious superstition for a short time, but it broke out afresh – not only in Judaea, where the plague first arose, but in Rome itself.'

The resurrection

Acts 17:22–32 ☐

When Paul proclaimed the resurrection in Acts 17:22–32, the listening Athenians mocked him. It is still the same today.

The resurrection was a miraculous event which cannot be explained 'scientifically'. This means that some people dismiss the accounts without any thought. They have decided in advance that, whatever the evidence, nobody can rise from the dead. Many other people, however, have more open minds, and there is plenty of evidence for the resurrection which we can pass on to convince them.

Matthew 28:1–8 ☐

Mark 16:1–8 ☐

Luke 24:1–10 ☐

John 20:1–8 ☐

1 Corinthians 15 ☐

The New Testament contains five accounts of the resurrection: Matthew 28:1–8; Mark 16:1–8; Luke 24:1–10; John 20:1–8 and 1 Corinthians 15. Some people argue that these accounts contradict each other, but there are two basic principles behind the differences between the accounts (and the other differences between the Gospels).

1.   *incompleteness*

No Gospel tries to tell the whole story, describe all the details, introduce all the characters, and so on. They look at events strictly from one perspective, so that we have a series of descriptions of the same events from different viewpoints. This means that looking at the Gospels is rather like looking at a mountain from the four points of the compass: the aspects are different though it is all the same mountain.

John 20:2 ☐

John, for example, mentions Mary Magdalene, Salome and Mary the wife of Cleopas at the cross, but only Mary Magdalene at the tomb. Yet the plural in 20:2 shows that Mary was not alone – it is just that John has not mentioned them.

Luke 24:12 ☐
        24:24 ☐

It is the same in Luke. In 24:12, it seems that only Peter went to the tomb, but 24:24 shows that others did too. When a Gospel mentions only one name, it does not imply that the writer was unaware that others were present. Instead, it is merely focusing attention on a particular person.

2.   *telescoping*

Acts 1:3 ☐

In Luke, it seems that Jesus' resurrection appearances and ascension took place on the same day. Yet in Acts (which was also written by Luke) it is clear that the events were spread over forty days. Luke has merely telescoped the events to bring out a particular perspective.

Matthew's Gospel uses the same literary device in the events of the angel's descent and his conversation with the women.

Once we grasp these two principles, we can see that the five accounts of the resurrection fit together in exactly the kind of way that historians expect of eye-witness accounts, and that they contain many corroborating cross-details which would be hard to invent.

The accounts make two simple claims:

- *Jesus' physical body disappeared from the tomb*

- *the risen Christ appeared to his followers*

People who mock the resurrection need to provide an alternative explanation for these two phenomena. Through the ages, a host have been suggested – and most are less plausible than the Christian explanation of a supernatural miracle.

Some people say that the accounts are *legendary*. But they do not read like first century myths; they bear all the hallmarks of independent accounts of actual events; and they were written within a few decades of the events.

Other suggest that it was simply a *mistake*, and the disciples went to the wrong tomb. But the women watched the burial; Joseph knew his family grave; the soldiers would not have guarded the wrong tomb; and the authorities would have quickly produced the real body.

A few argue that the body must have been *stolen*. But ordinary thieves would not have left the clothes and spices, nor would they have got past the guards; and the authorities would have had no reason to steal the body – except to *disprove* the resurrection stories.

Most opponents maintain that it must have been a *conspiracy*: either Jesus arranged for a substitute to be executed or for a soldier to cut him down before he died; or the disciples stole the body. But the crucifixion was too public for a substitute and the soldiers were too experienced to be fooled. And even if Jesus was not dead when he was sealed in the tomb, he would have been in no state to appear as a risen, glorious Lord within a few days!

The difficulty with the different conspiracy theories is that they mean Christianity must be based on an enormous lie. If this were true, would the disciples have been willing to face death for their belief in the resurrection? None of the theories explain how a group of frightened fishermen, who had just lost their leader, could have founded a new religion and fabricated such convincing accounts of actual events!

Finally, a few sceptics put it all down to mass *hallucination*. But the disciples were not expecting anything to happen, for they thought it was all over. People do not take burial spices to a tomb if they are expecting the body to be resurrected, nor do they assume that the body must have been moved by the authorities. And an hallucination could not eat a piece of grilled fish, or be prodded and poked.

The problem with most of the alternative explanations is that they do not explain the resurrection appearances; the problem with hallucination is that it does not explain the missing body. And the resurrection cannot have been both a conspiracy *and* an hallucination!

None of the alternative ideas make sense. All that is left is the belief that the accounts describe actual events as the eye-witnesses saw them. Christ is risen, not just in the sense of 'his ideas live for ever', but in the fact that his actual person lives and relates to people today. This is the gospel, and it is reasoned, logical good news.

A LIFE-CHANGING MESSAGE

In *Knowing the Father*, we consider the cross from the Father's point-of-view; in *Knowing the Son*, we examine it from Jesus' perspective; and in *Salvation by Grace* we study the ideas and images which the New Testament uses to explain its achievements.

Here, however, we consider the cross from our human perspective to see how the lives of lost people are changed by God through the cross.

The damage of sin

Jesus came into the world to reverse the consequences of humanity's fall in Eden; he came to remedy the creature's rebellion against the Creator, which is reported in Genesis 3, and bring total reconciliation.

When Adam and Eve sinned, humanity was bound by-and-to Satan. They lost the freedom of the children of God because they rejected God's rule and replaced it with Satan's. From that moment, the world began to be dominated by Satan. As a result of their sin, humanity became guilty. It was placed under God's wrath, and this led to the punishment in this life of increased suffering and sweat; and, in the life to come, of hell.

People became alienated from each other because of their embarrassment and shame at their shortcomings. When Adam and Eve made a futile attempt to cover their nakedness and hide, they were simply too ashamed to face God. They took their shame with them when they left Eden, and this affected their relationships with other people. Sin always ultimately results in this sense of shame; and human attempts to cover it, or to hide it, fail to deal with the shame.

The wage of the first sin was spiritual death. Adam and Eve forfeited the privilege of close fellowship with God, which is eternal life, and were expelled from his presence.

The damage undone

On the cross, Jesus dealt with all this. He died to rescue humanity from Satan's grip, and decisively defeated him by his perfect submission to the Father and his absolute moral perfection. Jesus died and rose again as the victor who destroys Satan's last weapon, death. And, by his own death, he established the rightful rule of God and set the world free.

Through his death, Jesus also made atonement for the sin of the whole world and earnt its forgiveness. On the cross, he appeased God's wrath, satisfied God's holy nature, and delivered humanity from the guilt of sin. He died as the Saviour who voluntarily accepted our blame, endured the agony of separation from the Father, took the faults of many on himself, and won eternal redemption and reconciliation.

In his death, Jesus also left an example of the ideal way for men and women to live and die. Even while he suffered, he made time to show exemplary human behaviour in asking God to forgive those who were torturing him and in comforting a criminal with the promise of paradise. When he died as the ideal Human, Jesus left everything behind and committed his spirit into God's hands. On the cross, he provided for all time the perfect example of submissive obedience.

At the same time, Jesus also died on the cross in excruciating pain to struggle and strain for the birth of a new creation. After six hellish

Psalm 42:1–2 ☐

Isaiah 53:10 ☐

hours of spiritual childbirth he was, like the panting deer of Psalm 42:1–2, deeply spiritually thirsty. As he died in labour, he could cry 'I've done it!' because, like the servant in Isaiah 53:10, he had seen his offspring. So Jesus went to the cross as the divine Parent to travail and give birth to a new creation which would reproduce the divine nature.

In our evangelism, we should speak about all these achievements, and not focus on one and ignore another. We need to address all humanity's basic problems and describe God's complete response in Christ. At the very least, we need to proclaim that people are:

- *in the grip of the world, the flesh and the devil, and unable to break free; but Jesus has broken the bondage, and now offers freedom*

- *guilty before God because of their sin, and unable to escape from this burden; but Jesus has willingly experienced God's anger in our stead, and now offers forgiveness*

- *ashamed and embarrassed in front of each other, and unable to relate well to others because of something which is fundamentally wrong; but Jesus brings complete understanding and perfect sympathy, and now offers comfort and companionship*

- *spiritually dead, and unable to resuscitate themselves; but Jesus has strained for the heavenly birth of each member of humanity, and now offers eternal life freely to all*

- *in rebellion against God, and needing to be brought into obedience; so God has provided Jesus as the king to whom all men and women must submit*

- *sinful, and needing someone to deal with that sin; so God has provided Jesus as the sacrifice who removes sin*

- *experiencing disunity and fragmentation, and needing to become whole, integrated, able to relate easily with others; so God has provided Jesus as the perfect example of wholeness, social integration and inter-personal relationships*

- *spiritually dead, and needing to receive light, life, truth and love from God; so God has provided Jesus as the source of these qualities*

There is only one gospel message, yet it has many aspects. And we need to explore those complementary sides which we neglect because of our background and experience. We may need to vary our proclamation to take account of the full message, and we should ensure that new believers grasp the greatness of the gospel – and experience all its aspects – so that they can grow strong, balanced and whole.

A RELEVANT AND REASONED MESSAGE

When we start to speak to people about Jesus, and to introduce them to the wonder of God's grace and the great achievements of the cross, we often find that they raise issues which they consider to be insurmountable objections to the Christian faith.

There are a whole series of questions which modern men and women constantly ask, and we need to be able to answer them in a relevant and reasoned manner. It is not possible to deal here with every question which is commonly asked, but we can think about some of the general issues which seem to be particularly relevant today.

Suffering

Many unbelievers do not consider it rational to believe that a God of love could create a world which is as full of pain as ours. They think suffering proves that God must be impotent, sadistic or callous.

We believe, however, that God is all-loving, and that he wanted to create beings with whom he could enjoy a reciprocal love-relationship. Without freedom of choice, love would be meaningless. We can have a two-way love relationship with a person who has free-will, but not with an automaton who obeys our every whim.

If we possess free will, we must also possess the possibility of rejecting God, going our own way, and inflicting harm. This means that the possibility of suffering is inherent in the existence of freedom.

When the first human beings rejected God, they did not choose an entity called evil which God had already made. Instead, in the act of choosing, they created their own evil. When we construct a box, we do not need to find some darkness to fill it; instead, we need only to shut out the light. So, whenever humanity excludes the light and love of God, it automatically 'creates' the darkness and pain of evil.

Despite this, people are always asking, 'Why doesn't God do something? Why doesn't he stop war, end starvation, prevent accidents, abolish disease, and so on?' They do not realise that, if God were to stop all the trouble and evil in the world, he would be compelled to eradicate free people too – for we are filled with the selfishness which is the source of most suffering.

But God has not done nothing. Instead of removing human freedom, he has sent Jesus to deal with human sin, to show people how to live, and to offer humanity both the possibility of choosing good and rejecting evil and the spiritual strength to overcome selfishness.

Some people try to insist that God's wisdom and power means he should have created free beings who were certain to resist temptation and always do good, but this is nonsense. Suffering is the *inevitable* price of freedom, and it is humanity's abuse of free will which has led to evil and which still leads to most of the suffering in the world.

If God intervened to correct every abuse of free will he would have to create a world where wrong actions and thoughts were impossible, a world without freedom. Although God does occasionally interrupt our free will in order, for example, to do a very extraordinary miracle, he generally respects humanity's freedom – as this contains the possibility of the love that he prizes above all else.

Some people wonder whether the suffering we see is too high a price for the love God seeks, but we cannot evaluate this. We cannot weigh an hour of love against an hour of pain. As far as the Bible is concerned, present sufferings cannot be compared with future glory.

This explanation of suffering may not satisfy everyone, but this should not deter us from proclaiming the claims of the one who himself suffered on the cross, and bore the full pain of evil, so that we can be reconciled to God in the loving relationship he has always intended.

God the Creator

There is always someone who thinks that they are the first person to ask, 'Who made God?' and to wonder what he was doing before the world began.

Since Einstein, we know that time can bend, slow down or speed up when things travel at very high speeds. This is hard to grasp, but it does make it easier to accept the biblical teaching that God is beyond time. If God is outside time, it is meaningless to ask when he began, how he was made, and what occupied him. These sorts of questions make the false assumption that God exists within time, and are no different from asking when King Alfred met Tony Blair.

Many people do not bother with these questions because they are sure 'everybody knows' that belief in God has been discredited by what they call 'science'. For them, believing in a Creator is on the same level as believing in a flat earth or a cheese moon. This might be a common position, but it is astonishingly ignorant.

There are only three logical theories about the origin of the universe:

a) *Matter and energy have always existed; they are the ultimate reality: life and the time-space universe are the results of their totally random activity.*

b) *Matter and energy spontaneously came into being out of nothing, without – by definition – any cause or explanation.*

c) *A wholly-other, wholly-beyond, wholly non-material spiritual being created space, time, matter, energy and life.*

On rational grounds, (b) is incredible – which leaves two logically equal possibilities. But belief in (a) involves a serious problem, for the current scientific understanding of thermo-dynamics insists that, *given infinite time*, the energy levels within a closed system will become uniform, and all energy and matter will reduce to their simplest forms. As energy levels are manifestly not uniform in our universe, either (a) is untenable or current scientific knowledge is deeply flawed.

The common criticism of (c) is that this merely moves the question back one stage, but this is not true. A material world may be subject to time and the laws of thermo-dynamics, but a spiritual God is not.

If matter is *all* that exists, critics must explain either why it has not run down or how nothing can have become something. But if there is a beyond-time, beyond-matter, spiritual God, it is meaningless to ask how he started and unnecessary to ask why he has not run down.

Other religions

Many people insist that all religions lead to God, and that Christians are insufferably arrogant to suggest otherwise. But all roads do not lead to Scotland, all trains do not go to London and all planes do not fly to Africa.

If Scotland, London and Africa all renamed themselves Scotlonca it might become accurate to say that all journeys lead to *a* scotlonca, but people who wanted to reach the African Scotlonca would be very disappointed if they caught a train in Birmingham!

It is the same with the different world religions. The fact that they all refer to a god does not mean that they are all describing the same being or are all moving towards the same destination. The Hindu religion, for example, believes that God is in both good and evil things, while there is no all-powerful being in most branches of Buddhism. As most religions use the word 'God' to refer to entirely different concepts, it is absurd to suggest that they must all lead to the same person.

We should be wary about rehearsing our questions, but it can be helpful to ask people to describe the God in whom they do not believe, and the One to whom they think all religions lead.

We can usually point out that we also do not believe in such a 'God', and that we are not travelling towards the 'One' they describe. We can then go on to introduce them to *Yahweh*, the living God of the Bible, who has perfectly revealed himself in Jesus.

The Bible

There is a widespread idea that the Bible is about as relevant as Grimm's Fairy Tales. Most people seem to think that the Bible has been disproved by science, archaeology and history, that it is just a collection of old myths and propaganda, and that the two Testaments present opposite pictures of God.

The problem is that people's ideas about the Bible are usually based on what they think the Bible says rather than what it really says. Although people may refer to a few superficial matters like Adam's navel and Balaam's donkey, the real issue is always 'inspiration'.

For ourselves, we need to be completely clear what the Bible teaches about its inspiration. For example:

• *it is not a book of 'magic' sayings*

When we insist that God inspired the whole Bible we are not saying that everything in the Bible is inspired. For example, the recording of the words of Job's comforters is inspired, but what they said is not;

and when the Bible records the saying, 'There is no God', it is the act of recording not the saying itself which is inspired.

- *it is not a textbook of absolute rules*

The Bible records how the living God related to living people in different ways according to their historical and moral conditions. For example, the Law of Moses permitted divorce, but Jesus said that this had only been included in the Law because the people had hard hearts.

Of course, there are some absolute rules which are repeated throughout the whole Bible (it is always wrong to covet), but not everything is of this nature.

- *out of context statements can be misunderstood*

When, for example, God told Abraham to sacrifice Isaac, he did not intend this to be done. It was a genuine word from God, but we cannot build a doctrine of human sacrifice on it. The real story is about testing and strengthening Abraham's faith.

- *it is not a Western style textbook of history or science*

The Bible is a Middle Eastern book which tries to teach the significance of history and to introduce the Person behind all scientific 'laws'. It is more concerned with style, understanding, principles and significance than with precise details of exact chronology and scientific causality. We must watch that we are not so pre-occupied with a poetic detail that we miss the profound truth it is trying to illustrate.

- *the full revelation of God is not included in every part of the Bible*

There is a gradual building up of the picture of God through the Bible, a progressive unveiling which leads to Jesus. The Old Testament continually 'foreshadows' God's Son, the Messiah, and the two Testaments can be understood accurately only in the light of each other. The New deepens and extends what has been established in the Old – it neither replaces or repeats its revelation.

Many people suggest that the Old Testament presents a God of wrath and that the New depicts a God of love. Yet Jesus encapsulates the Old Testament Law in its command to love God and others; he points out that God, through the prophets, continually called for love and mercy rather than sacrifice and ceremony; and he himself warned people about 'hell-fire'.

The God of the Bible is a living person who deals with people personally according to their different real-life situations. At times, this leads to different emphases, but we can see from Genesis to Revelation that God is unchanged in his attitude of grace and love to humanity.

When we read the Bible in the way that it was intended, and make sense of each passage according to its literary form, we see the same God on every page and are not confused by a modern Western approach to literature.

Sensible answers

The stories of Abram, Job and Habakkuk show that God likes people who are prepared to be real with him and to ask him about the questions which deeply matter to them – he always responds to honest searchers after truth.

As God's heralds, we are an important part of this process, and we need to grapple with the issues of the day so that we can pass on God's answers to peoples' questions about miracles, church disunity, Christian hypocrisy, sin, suffering, the meaning of life, and so on.

Our answers, however, must be reasoned and reasonable. We know that our Christian faith is a relationship of trust and not just a set of logical beliefs, but we must also recognise that Jesus and the apostles did not reject knowledge, logic and reason. For example:

- *they argued logically about doctrines and expected their teachings to make sense* – Matthew 5:46; 6:30; 7:11, 16; Romans 2:1; 1 Corinthians 6:2; Galatians 2:14

- *they appreciated the value of eye-witnesses* – John 15:27; 1 Corinthians 15:5–8

- *they argued and disputed with unbelievers, starting from their listeners' assumptions* – Acts 9:22, 29; 17:2–4, 17; 18:4, 19, 28

- *they urged us to prepare answers* – 1 Peter 3:15

In our increasingly pagan society, it is imperative that we take this advice and ensure that our message is as sharp and well-reasoned as possible, and that we have adequate answers to people's questions.

Matthew 5:46 ☐
6:30 ☐
7:11–16 ☐
Romans 2:1 ☐
1 Corinthians 6:2 ☐
Galatians 2:14 ☐
John 15:27 ☐
1 Corinthians 15:5–8 ☐
Acts 9:22–29 ☐
17:2–4 ☐
17:17 ☐
18:4, 19 ☐
18:28 ☐
1 Peter 3:15 ☐

A PERSONAL MESSAGE

Even though we should be able to debate and discuss human ideas and questions with academic detachment, we must never forget that God's heraldic message has dynamic personal implications.

When the apostle Paul evangelised in Athens, he not only amused the crowds with news of the resurrection, he also upset them by insisting that God commanded them to repent. We see this in Acts 17:21–30.

Acts 17:21–30 ☐

God does not send us as his heralds because he is interested in cerebral ideas; instead, he sends us with his message because he is concerned with reaching the lost, saving the world, changing human lives and healing broken relationships.

Related to experience

Whenever Paul spoke about Jesus' death and resurrection, he always related it to his personal experience. Like him, we need to stress that the cross is central to the Scriptures, rooted in history, logical, reasonable and packed with profound truths. But we also need to show that it works, that *we have seen the Lord* and *know him personally*.

Our authority as a herald does not lie in the way we deliver the message, understand it fully and have convincing answers; our authority lies in knowing the king, being changed by his power and enabled by his Spirit. We see this personal element in passages like 1 Corinthians 15:3–58; 2 Peter 1:16–18 and 1 John 1:1–3.

1 Corinthians
15:3–58 ☐

2 Peter 1:16–18 ☐

1 John 1:1–3 ☐

Demands a response

Matthew 10:34 shows that Jesus' words and presence always divide people. His claims are so absolute, his commands so authoritative, his teaching so unequivocal, that people are either for him or against him. They either respond to him with a 'Yes', or reject him with a 'No'. There is no 'grey' area, no halfway position, no ambivalence.

Matthew 10:34 ☐

On the day of Pentecost, at the end of the first evangelistic sermon, the crowd responded, in Acts 2:37, with a question, 'What shall we do?' True proclamation of the king's gospel message still demands a human response, and the biblical response is clear.

Acts 2:37 ☐

- *repent*

- *believe*

- *be baptised*

- *receive the Holy Spirit*

We consider this fourfold response in some detail in *The Rule of God* and *Glory in the Church*; and we study belief in *Living Faith*, baptism in *Glory in the Church*, and receiving the Spirit in *Knowing the Spirit*. In summary, though:

Repentance is total revolution, a radical change of mind, which results in a change of direction. It is not only a negative turning from wrong attitudes and actions, it is also a positive turning to God and his way of thinking and living.

Belief involves a clear commitment to the will of the Father and the person of Jesus. It involves intellectual assent, but goes much further. It is gospel obedience; it is total surrender to the rule of God; it is a dedication to lifelong discipleship.

Baptism is God's oath, his covenant sign, which seals the essential blessings of the gospel: cleansing from sin, union with Christ, death to the old and resurrection to the new, consecration to God, participation in Sonship, membership of the body of Christ.

Receiving the Spirit is an essential part of the good news, for it is through receiving him that we are born again into God's family and begin to enjoy God's presence, and it is through being baptised in him that we are empowered to live God's life and serve him with divine effectiveness.

This fourfold response is part of Jesus' gospel. He called people to repent, to believe, to be baptised, and to wait for the Spirit whom he would send. And he called them to follow him as part of a body of disciples. On through Acts, the early church proclaimed the same message – except that people now followed Jesus within the fellowship and life of the church, and they no longer had to wait for the Spirit because Jesus had sent him.

A unique message

There is only one path to God, and that is through Jesus; we have seen, however, that this can be described in many complementary ways.

For example, Jesus adapted his words and images to make them relevant to his hearers. He used everyday pictures to present the good news in a way which was meaningful to ordinary hurting people. He spoke about the gospel in terms of farming, building, fishing, gardening, cooking, sewing, shepherding, buying, selling, drinking, eating, and so on.

Paul inventively used the language of the law courts, the slave market and family life to describe the achievements of the cross in a way which communicated with the ordinary people of his day.

And, in the book of Acts, the apostles laced their messages with scriptural references and allusions when they were talking to Jews; but hardly referred to the Old Testament when preaching to Gentiles – instead, they mentioned heathen tombs and Greek poets.

This suggests that we must be totally faithful to the essence of the gospel – to the biblical Christ, to his death and resurrection, to his achievements on the cross – in our verbal proclamation of the king's message; but that we must work hard to be flexible, relevant and creative in the way we present it to the lost and hurting people whom we have been anointed to reach.

PART FIVE

personal evangelism

In Matthew 6:25–26 and 10:29–31, Jesus stresses the great value of each individual person: every man, woman and child is known intimately by God and valued very highly. And in Luke 15:1–32 Jesus reveals the tremendous heavenly interest in reaching and saving lost individuals.

As God present-in-person, Jesus demonstrated this divine care and interest by the remarkable way that he reached out to individual people and related to them.

The Gospels describe the loving attention that he personally gave to individuals – a thief, a prostitute, a fisherman, a leper, a rich ruler, a crippled woman, a sick child, a grieving mother, a corrupt official, and so on. He cared for them all, but especially for the *ptochos*.

Jesus and men

No Gospel pays more attention to the relationships between ordinary men and Jesus than Luke. Matthew's Gospel mentions the Wise Men, and John's Gospel introduces Lazarus, Nicodemus and the beggar

Matthew
6:25–26 ☐
10:29–31 ☐

Luke 15:1–32 ☐

who wiped spittle from his face; but Luke's Gospel offers unique insights into Cleopas, Herod, Simeon, Simon, Zacchaeus, Zacharias, seventy disciples, the shepherds, and the thief on the cross.

Luke emphasises that Peter, James and John are particularly close to Jesus: these are the apostles whom he mentions most often. After the list in 6:12–16, Luke refers again only to these three, Levi and Judas. Luke shows that Jesus had more than twelve followers by referring to disciples *and* apostles. 6:13 shows that the disciples were a large group of men and women from whom the twelve apostles were chosen.

Luke records much more about Jesus' dealings with the great mass of ordinary disciples than with the twelve apostles, and 10:1–20 reports that seventy of the disciples were sent by Jesus to evangelise – and that they came back rejoicing.

Luke describes Jesus eating with two contrasting groups of men. Scribes, Pharisees and lawyers wined and dined Jesus, but only to catch him out; whereas tax-collectors and sinners hosted receptions to evidence their friendship and support. Luke records five meals where Jesus is a guest, and shows how Jesus challenged the social expectations. We see this in 5:32; 7:36–50; 11:37–54 and 14:1–14.

Throughout the Gospel, Luke introduces a series of men who respond to Jesus in contrasting ways. Many oppose Jesus vigorously; others rejoice in his grace and authority; and some turn away disappointed – unable to meet his demands.

Luke places ordinary men at the centre of the nativity; he presents Gentile men – especially centurions and soldiers – in a particularly favourable light; and he focuses on the involvement of ordinary men in the events around Jesus' death.

The Gospel begins with a detailed description of God's dealings with Zacharias and ends by recounting Jesus' long conversation with Cleopas. These two men, together with Zacchaeus, are Luke's main examples of *ptochos* men who are transformed by God.

The story of Jesus' personal evangelistic encounter with Zacchaeus, in 19:1–10, immediately follows his meeting with the rich young ruler in Luke 18:18–23. Their responses are offered as direct contrasts, and illustrate Jesus' parables in 16:19–31 and 18:9–14: the ruler could not meet Jesus' demands for great generosity, but the tax collector volunteers more than anyone can expect.

The story of Zacchaeus is typical of Luke, and ties together all his Gospel's themes. It includes repentance, generosity, hospitality, the lost and joy. Its powerful conclusion, in 19:10, is both the climax and the main theme of Luke's Gospel. We can learn much about effective personal evangelism from Jesus' example here.

Luke 19:10 ☐

Jesus and women

Luke's Gospel also pays special attention to the relationships between ordinary women and Jesus. The other Gospels mention women mainly in passing, while Luke records nineteen incidents which illustrate the way that women responded to Jesus.

In an age which dismissed women as insignificant chattels, Luke's Gospel reveals the revolutionary way that Jesus treated them. It shows, for example, how women:

- *featured in Jesus' parables – 15:8–10; 18:1–8*

- *were central to his nativity – 1:26 – 2:51*

- *were healed by him – 8:40–56; 13:10–17*

- *were accepted and forgiven by him – 7:36–38*

- *provided for Jesus – 8:1–3; 10:38–42*

- *were listened to by him – 11:27–28*

- *were commended by him – 21:1–4*

- *were filled with the Spirit – 1:41*

- *stayed with Jesus at his death – 23:49*

- *wanted to care for his body – 23:55*

- *were the first witnesses to the resurrection – 24:6*

Luke 15:8–10 ☐
18:1–8 ☐
1:26–2:51 ☐
8:40–56 ☐
13:10–17 ☐
7:36–38 ☐
8:1–3 ☐
10:38–42 ☐
11:27–28 ☐
21:1–4 ☐
1:41 ☐
23:49 ☐
23:55 ☐
24:6 ☐

Luke 7:11–16 illustrates Jesus' extraordinary patience and compassion with women. By touching the open coffin, Jesus made himself ritually unclean; it seems that showing his care for, and his identification with, the bereaved widow was more important.

Luke 7:11–16 ☐

The healing of the crippled woman, in 13:10–17, is a typical Luke story. It features a woman, records precise details about her condition and healing, mentions confrontation with the authorities, reports that

Luke 13:10–17 ☐

the woman glorified God, and ends by noting the people's rejoicing. This story, almost more than any other, reveals Jesus fulfilling the chief purpose of his anointing and reaching the *ptochos* with a demonstration of the gospel. It is a classic example of personal evangelism.

John's Gospel

John's Gospel is quite different from the other three Gospels. It concentrates more on worship; relates Jesus' life to the Jewish religious year rather than historical events; reports his teaching in the Temple rather than his parables by the way-side; and offers some carefully selected snapshots of Jesus' story from the sacred festivals rather than weaving the whole story around Jesus' journeys.

John 2:13–4:54 □

In John 4, for example, the story of Jesus' personal evangelistic encounter with a Samaritan women is set in the 2:13–4:54 context of celebrating the Passover, and is part of a progression of spiritual ideas based around the Passover theme. In 2:20, John stresses that the Son can restore whatever humanity ruins; next he introduces, in 3:3, the new birth; and then, in 4:14, the indwelling Spirit.

The stories of Jesus' personal evangelism with Nicodemus and the Samaritan woman are used to illustrate these spiritual themes. Despite all his religion, Nicodemus needs new life. And, despite all her sin, a defiled Samaritan can contain a spring of living water.

Because John focuses on Jewish feasts, his Gospel records only about twenty days in Jesus' ministry. Interestingly, however, a remarkable proportion of this describes Jesus' dealings with individuals. In John 4, for example, Jesus' encounter with the woman occupies thirty verses, while the subsequent Samaritan 'revival' is dealt with in four verses.

This should help us to realise that, alongside our 'new creation' passion for the *kosmos*, we must also care deeply for individual men and women – and should relate to them in the same sympathetic, attentive, affectionate and unpatronising way as Jesus.

When it comes to evangelism, however, many modern congregations concentrate on trying to reach crowds of people at formal, organised meetings. Jesus' example should convince us that personal evangelism by individual believers must be central to every church's mission of reaching the lost with the gospel of Christ.

A right focus on personal evangelism, however, should not cause us to overlook passages like Matthew 4:25; 8:1; 9:8, 33–36; 12:15, 23; 13:1, 34; and 14:13–23 which show that Jesus also ministered to vast multitudes of men and women.

Matthew 4:25 ☐
8:1 ☐ 9:8
9:33–36 ☐
12:15, 23 ☐
13:1, 34 ☐
14:13–23 ☐

It is important to realise that Jesus never actively sought these crowds; instead, they sought him. They flocked to inconvenient locations at unsociable times. They descended on a home where a miracle had occurred or they knew Jesus to be. Although this is increasingly common in Africa, Asia and Latin America, we currently experience little like this in western Europe.

Most of the Gospels, however, are taken up with describing Jesus' ministry at informal gatherings by the roadside, in homes and gardens, at meals and funerals, by a pool or in a boat.

Of course, Jesus did minister at formal, organised meetings in local synagogues; but these were not the focus of his evangelism. Jesus never ignored the crowds, and he did not neglect formal services; but the Gospels make it clear that personal, individual ministry was the heart of his evangelistic activity.

Jesus' personal evangelism did not follow a mechanical pattern. As we see throughout this *Sword of the Spirit* series, Jesus did nothing on his own initiative. He was perfectly submitted to the Father; he followed his instructions at all times; and he depended completely on his anointing with the Holy Spirit.

As we see in *Ministry in the Spirit* and *Listening to God*, if we are to share in Jesus' ministry and minister with his effectiveness, we too must submit to the Father's will, listen to his voice, follow his instructions with gospel obedience, and rely fully on the Spirit's enabling and equipping.

Although we are not called to imitate the exact details of Jesus' style and pattern of ministry, we can learn much about personal evangelism from the way that Jesus reached the lost.

We have seen that Jesus' meeting with Zacchaeus is a climactic moment in Luke's Gospel, and that his conversation with the Samaritan woman sets the scene in John's Gospel. Although these two stories are very different, and the people involved are social opposites, they contain five basic principles of personal evangelism which run through Jesus' ministry to the lost.

1. MAKE CONTACT

So far as we can tell, Jesus had not met either Zacchaeus or the woman before: the two stories seem to describe evangelistic encounters with complete strangers. In both cases, Jesus was on a journey: he was walking to Jerusalem when he passed through Jericho; and he was travelling to Galilee when he reached Sychar.

This shows that many of the best opportunities for personal evangelism occur in natural, everyday settings: on trains and planes, in supermarkets and cafes, in the park and at sports events, and so on.

From a human perspective, Jesus did not need to make contact with either person. He could have stayed at an inn in Jericho and pulled himself a drink from the well at Sychar. But Jesus was in touch with God and in love with people. He was alert to the Spirit's prompting and aware of people's deep need for salvation.

If we are to make effective gospel contact with people, we must genuinely want to reach them *and* we must listen to God for his leading.

There were significant social and racial obstacles at the well in Sychar, but Jesus' compassionate humanity enabled him to overcome the woman's suspicion and mistrust. Whereas, in Jericho, Jesus was faced with a crowd of curious people, and the Spirit showed him which one person to contact.

In both cases, Jesus made contact by putting himself in the person's debt. He asked the woman for a drink and the man for a bed. Many believers try to make contact with people today by offering to give something away. But Jesus made contact by doing the opposite. He took the lower place; he made a request; he asked a favour.

This approach to evangelism takes time, and carries a greater risk of rejection. But what does it really matter if we are ignored or rejected? Too often, it is our fearful pride which stops us from reaching people.

If we are to make contact with ordinary lost people, we must listen attentively to God, we must seek the Holy Spirit's clear leading, and we must be ready to suffer some of Jesus' pain and rejection. The closer we are to him, the more his motivating love can reach through us to the lost people we meet.

2. AROUSE CURIOSITY

It is instructive that Jesus did not 'preach' to Zacchaeus or the woman. Nor did he quote biblical texts, make a clichéd presentation of the gospel, or ask prepared questions which he had learned by rote.

The woman had clearly never heard of Jesus, so Jesus aroused her curiosity by *hinting* at something which was more satisfying than her present experience: we see this in John 4:10–14.

John 4:10–14 ☐

Jesus used creative words and images which were based in their immediate situation, and used an analogy of the gospel which was directly relevant to the woman's needs. As a result, the woman started to ask Jesus questions and to seek his help.

It was different with Zacchaeus. He had heard about Jesus from other people and was already curious. But nothing could have prepared him for the moment when Jesus addressed him by name when Zacchaeus thought that he was safely hidden in a tree!

This was probably a word of knowledge from the Spirit (though Jesus may have heard about Zacchaeus from Matthew). Spiritual gifts often arouse people's curiosity, as do books, films, plays, worship, sacrificial service, and so on. But we must allow time for curiosity to develop into serious enquiry. It is pointless to answer questions which people are not asking, and to rush people towards a decision which they are not ready to make.

Spiritual hunger

The woman and Zacchaeus were both spiritually hungry – even if they would not have admitted this to themselves. Most people are; for this is the way that we have been made by God.

Of course, few people will admit that they are spiritually hungry – or even realise it. Unless we can bring people to the point where they are asking questions or requiring help, it is unlikely that they will listen to the good news when we try to share it.

We often concentrate on words in evangelism: we wonder what we should say. But people are not hungry for words, they are hungry for reality, for integrity, for a special quality of life and living.

When people gasped at Jesus' authority, they were not just acknowledging the truth of his words, they were also marvelling at the quality of his life which somehow endorsed and added to his words.

Most people are initially attracted to Christ by seeing his reality in a believer. They might see a dramatic change in a friend who has just become a Christian, or they may be impressed by somebody's life of selfless service, or they might be amazed by a miracle, or they may just sense Christ's presence in someone they meet.

No matter what arouses their curiosity, they want to know that it is real – and not fake or contrived – and they want to be sure that the person's inner life matches their outer appearance.

Zacchaeus was curious to see if Jesus was as good as he had heard. One glimpse of the Lord, one sound of his voice, and Zacchaeus knew that this was reality. He was ready to respond. And, after a few minutes' conversation with Jesus, the woman moved from hostile suspicion to spiritual openness.

We must remember that people are not converted to a doctrine, they are converted to Christ; and transparent, infectious, joyful Christ-like holiness is a key ingredient in personal evangelism.

3. OFFER A CHALLENGE

John 4:15 ☐

When, in John 4:15, the Samaritan woman was curious enough to ask for 'this water', Jesus did not leap in with a presentation of the gospel. Instead, he sensitively challenged the critical area in her life.

Many believers would have rejoiced when the woman asked for 'water', and would have pressed the living water upon her. Jesus, however, was always more concerned to make disciples than to collect converts; and he always challenged people with the discipleship issue which was at the heart of their lives.

For the woman, it was men. For Zacchaeus, it was money. But Jesus did not rebuke the women for her immorality, and he did not chastise Zacchaeus about his greed. Instead, he gently challenged them both about the critical issues in their respective lives. He told the woman to call for her husband, and he asked Zacchaeus to provide food and lodgings for thirteen people.

Jesus' anointing and openness to the Spirit enabled him to receive some of God's knowledge about the woman – but he mentioned it very carefully. In personal evangelism, God still gives anointed believers 'words of knowledge' about the people they are seeking to reach.

This is an important gift of the Spirit, and we should always be listening for these divine insights when we are talking with people. But we need the Spirit's gift of 'wisdom' to handle this information with Jesus' sensitivity and boldness. We consider this in *Knowing the Spirit*, *Ministry in the Spirit*, and *Listening to God*.

Throughout the Gospels, we see Jesus repeatedly challenging people about the cost of discipleship – for example, Matthew 8:18–22; Mark 8:34; Luke 5:8–11; 18:18–30; John 5:14; 8:11. This is a critical element in evangelism.

Matthew 8:18–22 ☐
Mark 8:34 ☐
Luke 5:8–11 ☐
18:18–30 ☐
John 5:14 ☐
8:11 ☐

But Jesus never followed a formula; instead, he challenged different people in different ways. He pin-pointed the one area which mattered the most to that person, and explained the demands of God's kingdom – often in a way which discouraged all but the most serious.

4. AVOID CONFUSION

At the critical point in both stories, just before the woman and Zacchaeus accepted the gift of salvation, a confusing diversion arose.

Jesus' challenge to the woman was a little too close for comfort, so – in John 4:20 – she raised a religious 'red herring'. And Jesus' words to Zacchaeus so outraged the crowd that – in Luke 19:7 – they started to murmur against him.

John 4:20 ☐
Luke 19:7 ☐

The Jews and Samaritans had different ideas about religion, especially about the right place of worship, and the woman was using this issue as a diversionary tactic. People still do the same today. They often ask questions about suffering, evolution, other religions, and so on, not because they care deeply about the answer, but merely to divert the conversation away from Christ's uncomfortable challenge.

John 4:21–24 ☐

Jesus did not ignore the woman's question, but he was not distracted by it. In John 4:21–24, he gently dealt with her confusion, and then he brought her back to the more-important spiritual issue.

As we have seen, we all need good answers to the common questions that people ask about suffering, other religions, evolution, miracles, life after death, and so on. We need to be able to deal – clearly, logically and succinctly – with these issues; but we must not allow questions about them to side-track the person from their own spiritual need.

It was different with Zacchaeus. The distraction did not originate with him, it came from the crowds, and it would have been easy for Jesus to focus on them. He could have tried to justify his words, or to argue with the crowds them, or to explain himself, or even to seek to convert them.

Instead, Jesus refused to be distracted from his focus, from needy Zacchaeus. He simply ignored the crowd's murmurings and stood silently – waiting for Zacchaeus to silence the crowds with his words.

This took enormous wisdom, but it shows again that conversion does not depend on our words. We do not need all the answers. We do not need to control the whole situation. God is quite capable of working in the person's life through the Spirit. Sometimes, our silence is the most eloquent way of dealing with a distraction.

5. ESTABLISH COMMITMENT

Luke 19:8 ☐

Zacchaeus' words in Luke 19:8 are not exactly a classical statement of faith. But Jesus knew the man's heart, and publicly announced that salvation had come to the house.

John 4:29 ☐
    4:42 ☐

And the woman's words, in John 4:29, do not really ring with positive assurance. Yet 4:42 shows that the woman soon moved on to appreciate that Jesus was the Christ, the Saviour of the world.

It is easy to look for a prescribed response, or to expect people to express their commitment in the same way that we once did. But Jesus looked to the heart, not to the external words, and brought both these people to a commitment to him which was meaningful to them.

John 4:25 suggests that the woman tried some more delaying tactics. She was trying to postpone the decision to a later date. People still do this today, but Jesus brought her face to face with himself – which is what we should always seek to do in every form of evangelism.

These encounters with Jesus were unique events for Zacchaeus and the woman. He was especially near to them: it was their day of destiny. To a great extent, they would either be saved that day, or never.

There seem to be just a few times in each person's life when Christ is this near. This means that every evangelistic opportunity is critical, and needs responsible handling. We must encourage people to commit themselves to Christ, without pressurising them in any way.

It is often helpful to ask the person whether they would like us to suggest a prayer which will help them begin to follow Christ, or whether they would prefer to read something and pray on their own.

Each individual must be helped individually, and in a way and with words which are relevant to their situation. It is important, however, to be *simple* and *specific*. Most people are muddled about spiritual things, and generalisations do not help them.

Of course, we need a clear grasp of the gospel before we can be simple. But we do not need to explain the doctrine of justification to lead someone to Christ. At its most basic, it is probably helpful to use a loose framework like this:

- *turn away from your sinful thoughts and deeds, and admit your need of Jesus* – Romans 3:23; 6:23; Isaiah 59:1–3

- *believe that Jesus has done everything for you* – Isaiah 53:5–12; 1 Peter 2:24; 3:18

- *count the cost of discipleship* – Mark 8:34–38

- *receive the Holy Spirit* – Luke 11:13; John 3:5–8

In Part Four, we considered the message that we are called to bear to the lost. But we do not need to explain every detail to each person. Instead, we need to pick those aspects which the Spirit draws to our attention, and to present them with relevant words and analogies.

It is important we recognise that Zacchaeus and the woman both started spreading the good news for themselves. New converts are often the most effective evangelists, and a fresh testimony is usually a powerful way of spreading the gospel.

John 4:25 ☐

Romans 3:23 ☐
6:23 ☐
Isaiah 59:1–3 ☐
53:5–12 ☐
1 Peter 2:24 ☐
3:18 ☐
Mark 8:34–38 ☐
Luke 11:13 ☐
John 3:5–8 ☐

PART SIX

church evangelism

We have seen that the *message* of evangelism is Christ, and that the *method* of evangelism is individual believers reaching out personally to the lost people around them. Now we need to recognise that the *means* of evangelism is always the church.

Some modern evangelism is separated from local churches. There are, however, two important reasons why this makes little sense.

- *the church is God's appointed means for spreading the gospel*

- *the evangelistic message is meant to call people to the body of Christ, to the community of believers with Jesus as its head*

In *Glory in the Church*, we establish that witness is the main work of the church. John 15:26–27 and Acts 1:8 report the church's calling to be Jesus' witnesses – in words, deeds and lifestyle – to the ends of the earth. And the church has always grown whenever ordinary believers have been equipped and released as witnesses.

John 15:26–27 ☐

Acts 1:8 ☐

Churches which do not burn with a passion for witness miss the whole point of their calling – to go and make disciples of Jesus in all nations.

The Greek word *martureo*, 'to witness' means 'to speak about what has been seen or heard'. In the New Testament it is mainly used to describe the witness to Jesus by:

- *the Father* – John 5:32; 8:18; 1 John 5:9–10

- *Jesus himself* – John 3:11; 4:44; 5:31

- *the Holy Spirit* – John 15:26; Hebrews 10:15

- *the Scriptures* – John 5:39; Hebrews 7:8, 17

- *the works of Jesus* – John 5:36; 10:25

- *prophets and apostles* – Acts 10:43; 23:11; 1 Corinthians 15:15

This emphasises that all the church's words and activities are meant to point people to Jesus: we are witnesses to him, not to ourselves, or even to our local church.

John 1:27 and 3:28–30 are particularly relevant. The church's goal must be to testify to Jesus, to attract people to him, to encourage them to follow him, to assist them to love him, and so on.

We must always remember, however, that we cannot witness effectively to Jesus in our own strength and ability. We need the help of the Holy Spirit. John 15:18 reminds us that he is 'The Witness', and we can witness effectively only as we allow him to work in our lives. In Acts 1:8, the disciples were told that they had to wait for the power of the Spirit to come upon them before they could be effective witnesses, and this is still true for the church today.

Evangelism is not a specialised activity which the church should carry out only occasionally – it should characterise everything that we say and do. The truth is that every church is always witnessing to Jesus; sadly, much of what we say and do brings him little glory and turns many people from him.

Some believers are surprised to discover that the Bible contains few appeals to witness after Matthew 28:18–20. This is because evangelism was somehow assumed in the early church, and it functioned without any techniques, programmes or special encouragement.

The book of Acts shows that the whole church evangelised all the time. Unlike today, early church evangelism was not coerced, reluctant, half-hearted, occasional and ineffectual; instead, it was automatic, spontaneous, continuous and contagious!

God is concerned with saving individuals and making disciples, but he is also concerned with building his church. As we establish in *Glory in the Church*, he wants us to become a new society, a living community, which reveals his glory in-and-to the world.

God's original purpose, and his ultimate aim, is that those he creates in his image should be a community of divine love. This means that, whenever people commit themselves to Christ, they should also commit themselves to his body, to the church. As we have noted, this is part of the significance of baptism.

In Acts 2:40–47, when Peter had told the crowds what to do, and they had obeyed him, the new converts devoted themselves to the apostles' teaching and to living in fellowship. They expressed their commitment to Christ by living in his body.

Acts 2:40–47 ☐

REVELATION

We have seen that the good news is part of God's self revelation. This means that, in evangelism, the church reveals God to the world. We know now that this revelatory process should include:

- *proclamation* – public preaching *and* personal testimony

- *demonstration* – healings, expelling demons, miracles

- *incarnation* – Christ-like living among the hurting

Throughout this *Sword of the Spirit* series, we have stressed the general scriptural principle that divine revelation comes in many complementary ways which always agree with each other.

For example, in *Living Faith*, we establish that God reveals his Word through both his Personal Word, Jesus, and his Written Word, the Scriptures, and these are always utterly consistent with each other. We also see that God's *rhema* words always conform to his *logos* Word – to Jesus and to the Bible – and to all other *rhema* words.

And, in *Listening to God*, we observe that God speaks to us in a variety of ways, but that he confirms his Word by speaking to us in several different ways which always agree with each other.

This principle of agreement also applies to evangelism. God purposes to reveal his good news about himself in-and-through the church by several complementary ways which agree with each other. This is why the church's proclamation is never enough – there must also be a demonstration and an incarnation which confirms, and conforms with, the gospel being proclaimed.

We see this in Jesus, who revealed God, and revealed the truth about God, by words, deeds and holy living. He announced the gospel verbally, demonstrated the message visually, and incarnated the same message victoriously.

And we see it in the *parakletos*, the Holy Spirit, who speaks God's words to us, empowers us to do God's deeds, and makes us more like Jesus in our actions and attitudes.

This means that every congregation must ensure that evangelism permeates every part of its life, and that it fully reveals the good news in three basic ways which complement and conform with each other.

1.   Proclamation

Acts 2:11 □

14–40 □

Acts 2:11 reveals that the church began in worship; while Acts 2:14–40 shows that it moved to preaching to spread the good news. The Spirit fell; the disciples worshipped; but the people were only 'cut to the heart' when they heard the Word proclaimed in the power of the Spirit.

Acts 4:4 □

It is the same in Acts 3. A man was healed by the power of the Spirit, he praised God, but Acts 4:4 reports that it was the proclamation of the Word which caused the people to believe.

Acts 4:8–12 □

8:4 □

19:8–20 □

The Bible shows that the early church took every opportunity to proclaim God's word; we see this, for example, in Acts 4:8–12; 8:4 and 19:8–20 – which records an outstanding example of Paul's devotion to the Word, and of the way that God honoured his devotion.

We have seen that every aspect of the church's evangelistic proclamation must be rooted in God's Word – in Scripture and in Christ – but that we need to communicate the king's message to the lost in words and images which are relevant to them.

The book of Acts uses at least fifteen different Greek words to describe the great variety of ways that the early church proclaimed God's Word.

For example, the early church:

- *euangelizo*, 'evangelised' – Acts 8:4
- *suncheo*, 'confounded' – Acts 9:22
- *anangello*, 'announced' – Acts 20:20
- *parakaleo*, 'exhorted' – Acts 2:40
- *ektithemi*, 'explained' – Acts 28:23
- *kerusso*, 'heralded' – Acts 10:37
- *peitho*, 'persuaded' – Acts 13:43
- *katangello*, 'preached' – Acts 17:13
- *sumbibazo*, 'proved' – Acts 9:22
- *diaphero*, 'published' – Acts 13:49
- *dialegomai*, 'reasoned' – Acts 17:2
- *laleo*, 'spoke' – Acts 13:42
- *parrhesiazomai*, 'spoke boldly' – Acts 9:27–29
- *didasko*, 'taught' – Acts 18:11
- *diamarturomai*, 'testified' – Acts 8:25

Acts 8:4 ☐
Acts 9:22 ☐
Acts 13:42 ☐
Acts 2:40 ☐
Acts 28:23 ☐
Acts 10:37 ☐
Acts 13:43 ☐
Acts 17:13 ☐
Acts 20:20 ☐
Acts 9:22 ☐
Acts 13:49 ☐
Acts 17:2 ☐
Acts 9:27–29 ☐
Acts 18:11 ☐
Acts 8:25 ☐

We have seen that the stereotypical modern church sermon does not conform to the biblical idea of heraldic gospel proclamation, and this rich Greek vocabulary shows that the early church proclaimed the good news in all sorts of ways. To a certain extent, it did not matter how they proclaimed – so long as they passed on the good news to the poor.

Somehow, local churches need to recapture this urgency, variety and creativity of gospel proclamation so that they can communicate effectively and relevantly with the lost in their local communities.

Obviously, this should include formal proclamation like evangelistic preaching, guest services, home meetings and dramatic presentations, but it should also include informal proclamation like street work, house-to-house visitation, debates, questions, and so on.

The most important element, however, in any church's proclamation is the personal testimony of ordinary believers who gossip the gospel over the garden fence and down the tower-block corridor. A church's evangelistic meetings will preach to the converted unless its members are genuinely in the world, reaching the lost, befriending the hurting, speaking about Jesus, demonstrating the good news and overflowing with God's life.

2.   Demonstration

In *Ministry in the Spirit*, we consider fully the way that the whole church is called to demonstrate the gospel in signs and wonders. For example, we establish in some detail that:

- *any believer can minister*

- *we all minister as lowly, humble servants*

- *it is a distinct spiritual activity*

- *leaders should equip all the members to minister*

- *the prophetic ministry is the foundation of ministry*

- *we must be discipled by the Holy Spirit, depend on his anointing, discern his agenda, and demonstrate his gifts*

- *we can learn to share with Jesus in his healing ministry*

- *we can learn to exercise Jesus' authority and cast out demons*

- *we can learn to speak with prophetic authority, and change situation through anointed words of blessing or judgement*

- *we can learn to pass on God's counsel*

Throughout the Gospels and Acts, the ministries of healing and deliverance are essential features of church evangelism. On their own, Jesus' miracles revealed God's compassion and power, but they also confirmed what he proclaimed. Jesus' actions illustrated his announcing; they showed that the kingdom of God had come among ordinary people in great power, and that it was wide open to everyone.

As well as ministering himself, Jesus also trained and sent the disciples and apostles to proclaim the kingdom of God *and* to heal the sick *and* to release people from demons. They went in pairs from village to village and served the people that they met – by announcing the good news *and* by ministering God's healing *and* by releasing people from the grip of evil.

The early Church kept these callings together. They proclaimed, and they healed, and they cast out demons. When someone was healed or released, a spoken explanation was offered which pointed to Jesus. We must pray and work hard to re-establish this pattern in churches today.

3. Incarnation

We know that Jesus lived among ordinary hurting people in a way which showed that God accepted and loved them. His healing ministry confirmed the good news that he taught about the kingdom, and it demonstrated the divine love that his living among them suggested.

Jesus moved among the *ptochos* to proclaim and to demonstrate the gospel. He did not come from heaven with all the splendour and public acclaim to which, as God, he was entitled. Instead, he identified with humanity by living as an ordinary man, and by being subject to the same pressures as everyone else. The Word became flesh. The gospel was lived. The good news was seen to apply to all the ordinary details of a stressful human existence.

Jesus lived in a way to which the hurting people could relate, and he was always available to them. He even befriended – without a hint of patronisation – those who were rejected by contemporary society.

This means that, today, a local church's evangelism cannot be entirely removed from this context of 'living the gospel among the hurting' without some distortion of the message.

Instead, local church evangelism should be set in the context of a corporate lifestyle, which facilitates the proclamation of the gospel by ensuring that the whole life of the church is focused on the hurting, is relevant to their needs, and is accessible to them.

PRACTICAL CONCERNS

If a local church wants to be characterised by effective biblical evangelism, it needs to address a host of practical issues. Although we can be guided by general scriptural principles, we need special guidance from the Spirit as to the best action in particular situations.

Mobilisation

In evangelism, as in every aspect of church life, it is the divinely-appointed function of the leaders to release and equip all the members to do the work of Jesus Christ.

The entire church on earth is Christ's body on earth, which means that his will and ministry must be done through the whole of his body. If *all* the members of a local church are not mobilised and released in personal evangelism, the lost will never be reached in that locality.

Mass mobilisation often requires a radical transformation – especially in churches which believe that the minister is meant to do everything. Experience shows, however, that believers can be mobilised by a mixture of prayer, teaching, encouragement and example.

But it cannot happen unless leaders delegate – and they do this only when they recognise that their primary calling and responsibility is to equip their members for the work of ministry.

Ephesians
4:11–12 ☐

Mass mobilisation in evangelism requires planning and encouragement. Members need to be given specific, purposeful jobs. They need to be trained and supervised; assessed and encouraged – and then given even greater responsibilities. There must be planning *and* partnership. This is merely Ephesians 4:11–12 in action.

Buildings

Every church has to meet somewhere. It may be a home, a hired hall or a building which has been a place of worship for centuries. If a local church is to reach the lost rather than the saved, it must think hard about where it should hold its evangelistic meetings.

Some traditional church buildings are no longer accessible to the general public. If the lost cannot get to a building easily, or if they do not know where it is, they will not come. If a building can be reached only by those who own cars, the elderly and the poor will be excluded.

Most non-Christian people in western Europe associate 'church' with a particular type of building, but new churches usually have to meet in schools, community halls, hotel rooms, and so on. These need to avoid looking like a strange sect and to ensure that their signs and publicity clearly identify them as a bona fide Christian group.

As far as possible, the buildings we use should be well-heated in winter and well-ventilated in summer; they should be well-lit, with comfortable seats. Non-Christian people like to go somewhere nice, so we should make the room we use as attractive as possible.

Some churches use OHP screens which are illegible to the people at the back and the elderly, and to everyone on a sunny day! Or they use so many books and leaflets that outsiders never know what page they are meant to be on. These sorts of details are important; if we really want to reach the lost, we will try to see how we appear to people in the locality – and take steps to rectify any problems.

Evangelistic meetings

Churches need to take care of all the details in their meetings – especially those which focus on the lost. We need to prepare thoroughly every aspect, trusting the Spirit to inspire us in advance.

We need to pray for God's guidance and blessing well beforehand. On their own, last minute prayers are simply not adequate. Of course, we should always be ready to adjust our plans at the last minute if it is plain that God has something different for us to do or say.

We should provide a good welcome for visitors, and quickly make them feel at ease – without ignoring or overpowering them. It is helpful to give them something which lets them know what is happening and gives them some facts about the church. If we genuinely want to reach them, we will contact them again in the following week.

No meeting should start late, contain too many items, or take too long. In many churches, there is a tendency for the sermon and worship to be too long, and so be off-putting to non-Christians.

It is far better to have one good hour of a high quality meeting – which leaves people wanting more – than two hours of an unstructured free-for-all which people find exhausting or tedious.

The style of meeting should be appropriate to the venue, culturally relevant to the people who attend, and inclusive. Many services contain too much jargon and too many phrases which are incomprehensible – or just plain silly – to non-Christians. We should always try to ensure that our language is simple, clear, accessible and sensible to newcomers.

The music in a meeting is bound to reflect the congregation's ethnic and cultural composition. But there should always be a place for 'churchy' music, as non-Christians feel more comfortable if there are some hymns which they know from their childhood.

Whatever style is used, we need constantly to explain our distinctives to newcomers. For example, the raising of hands, praying in tongues and shouting 'Hallelujah' can be culturally alienating. Yet a simple, brief explanation can break down these barriers.

We must try to create a relaxed atmosphere in our meetings, whilst ensuring that it is well structured. Everything in the meeting – the prayers, notices, songs, testimonies, readings, and so on – must be performed with excellence but without a clinical perfection.

Evangelistic sermons should be clear, relevant, simple, *and not too long!* We should learn from Jesus. He pointed to the flowers and talked about things which were relevant to the people in an agricultural society. We need to be equally relevant to our age and culture.

Of course, the presence of God is the most important thing that we can have in a meeting. An unbeliever can walk into a room which is cold, bare, badly equipped, and be touched by the presence of God. It is not because these things do not matter, it is merely that we can have beautiful carpets, superb equipment and be without God's power.

Evangelistic relationships

The corporate life of a church is as much a revelation of the gospel as a gripping sermon and a great healing. Local churches can start to build evangelistically attractive relationships by providing a variety of activities which help their members to have contact with each other, and with non-believers, outside the main services.

Whatever the size of its congregation, a church should provide a mixture of opportunities which help people to build relationships. For example, mid-week house-groups are often unattractive to men: we should recognise that women tend to be comfortable in homes but that most unsaved men prefer a pub, hotel room or sporting venue.

Every church needs a changing mixture of small groups, goal-directed activities, sporting activities, special interest groups – different opportunities for *inclusive* interaction. Like everything else, this takes creative thinking, constant encouragement and sensible planning.

We must remember that a church reveals God's passion for people through its corporate relationships. The church is all about God loving people, and good church relationships reveal to the lost the practical achievements of the cross like forgiveness and reconciliation.

Humans beings are extraordinary. They are unpredictable, argumentative and imperfect; but they are also funny, loveable and uniquely valuable. They are packed with divine potential – each one matters more than any project, any building, any meeting. We must love them without any qualifications or pre-conditions.

Of course, they may hurt and betray us, just as we may damage and disappoint them. But, if we let them, they will bless us, build the church, and reach the lost. If Jesus really did die for them, they must be worth every sacrifice that we can make – and many more.

We live in a society which continually devalues people. It isolates us socially. It strips us of our humanity. It makes us feel insignificant, unimportant, irrelevant. We all feel much better when we are treated with some respect and importance. The quality of our church relationships should – in this afflicted society – act like a powerful magnet drawing the hurting back to God's healing love.

Encouragement

Churches which succeed in reaching the lost are usually filled with encouragement. This should not surprise us for encouragement is the essence of the Holy Spirit. In fact, the Greek word for encouragement, *paraklesis*, is a form of the word that Jesus uses in John 16:7 to introduce the Spirit as the helper, advocate, comforter or *encourager*.

John 16:7 ☐

Encouragement means getting alongside people in exactly the same way that Jesus did – and as the Spirit does. It means gently but persistently urging people on in their lives with God.

Acts 4:36 shows how Joseph of Cyprus was given the 'nickname' Barnabas because he was such an encourager. Acts 11:24 describes Barnabas as 'full of the Holy Spirit', and Acts 9:26–28; 11:19–26; 12:25–13:5 show how he went alongside people to encourage them, train them and release them in evangelism.

Acts 4:36 ☐
11:24 ☐
9:26–28 ☐
11:19–26 ☐
12:25–13:5 ☐

If a local church claims to be filled with the Spirit, the *Parakletos*, it follows that it should be characterised by *paraklesis*. And if a church gives the *Parakletos* a special place and honour, encouragement should be its most dominant feature. This means that, if we care about people with the care of the Spirit, we will affirm them, build them, and do everything that we can to reach them, welcome them, train them and release them in personal evangelism.

Some leaders seem to think that their church would evangelise more effectively if only the members were more committed. They see the problem in terms of the people's lack of commitment. They are always telling their people that they do not pray enough, do not witness enough, do not give enough, and so on. Yet our God is characterised by grace, not condemnation.

We must not drive people too hard or too fast, lest they become resentful. Instead, we must let them go at their pace – we must be patient and work slowly but persistently. We need to recognise God's patience with us – how long he has put up with our funny ways and ideas, how long he has tolerated our faults and unhelpful habits. We should not expect people to change any quicker than we have!

Instead, we should remember the great evangelistic truth of John 17:21, and ask God to fill us with his love, his patience and his persistence; for, ultimately, it is the quality of our relationships – the depth of our love for one other – which will convince the *kosmos* of the truth about Jesus.

PART SEVEN

evangelism and discipleship

The great commission, in Matthew 28:18–20, is often quoted to justify all sorts of different evangelistic activities; yet this was not a divine instruction to preach 'gospel' sermons and make quick converts, it was a charge to make committed disciples.

We have seen that Jesus' gospel message was the kingdom, the personal rule of God. This means that, in his proclamation, the call to discipleship did not come after the call to Christ; rather, the call to Christ was itself a call to discipleship – it was all 'Follow me', and not a separate 'Follow up'. This shows that discipleship is an integral part of biblical evangelism, and not an optional extra tagged on afterwards.

The New Testament contains a few passages – like 1 Corinthians 1:1–2 and Hebrews 5:12–14 – which are aimed at disciples who were still 'babies in Christ'. This suggests that evangelism which does not include thorough discipleship is not just a modern phenomena!

Jesus was often distressed by his disciples' slowness to understand, their quickness to quarrel, and their weakness in faith. Nevertheless, he was committed to helping them develop as disciples by learning to recognise and trust God's personal rule.

Matthew
28:18–20 ☐

1 Corinthians
1:1–2 ☐

Hebrews
5:12–14 ☐

Acts 20:20, 31 ☐

Colossians
      1:28–29 ☐

1 Thessalonians
      2:7–12 ☐

The New Testament records the apostle Paul's determination to build churches which would stand firm against all opposition. Passages like, for example, Acts 20:20, 31; Colossians 1:28–29 and 1 Thessalonians 2:7–12 demonstrate that discipleship was a fundamental part of his evangelistic ministry. In fact, we can almost say that, for Paul, evangelism was not over until Ephesians 4:12–13 was well underway.

FIRST STEPS

A new relationship begins whenever a person starts to trust Jesus. The earnest desire of every new baby-Christian should be to make Jesus the ruler of every part of their life. If they have heard the news that he is the ideal *King* whom everyone needs, they should start to search God's Word regularly to grasp the principles on which to run their lives.

Hopefully, every new convert has also heard the message that salvation is a gift from God and that sinners can do nothing to save themselves. Once converts grasp this, they should stop trying to make amends for their sins and shortcomings, and start appreciating that their new relationship with their *Saviour* is based on the grace he shows towards people who can never earn or deserve his favour.

If they have heard the full gospel, new Christians should start to develop a personal relationship with their new *Friend*, who has been tempted in every way that they are without giving in to sin. Disciples who nurture this friendship discover that Jesus sympathises with their experiences because he has, in principle, been through them all himself.

And, if heralds have genuinely proclaimed the king's message – without omitting, altering or adding anything – new believers should start to worship the true *God*; not one of their own imagination, but the God who is the truth, the source of all life and love.

Sadly, many baby-Christians are not helped as they should be, and hear a less-than-complete gospel. God loves these impoverished people, and seeks to lead them into the fullness of the good news. Meanwhile, however, he expects us to lead people into the full light of his kingdom and into the full liberty which belongs by right to all his sons and daughters. He expects us to make real disciples.

Gospel obedience

In *Knowing the Father*, we see that God calls his disciples to accept his personal rule and commit themselves to living in gospel obedience: this is the first and most basic step of discipleship.

Gospel obedience is not a legalistic obedience to a set of rules; it is a disciplined, personal, enabled, moment-by-moment obedience to the Father himself. Living in the Father's grace means living in his will; and it is our gospel obedience which keeps us close to him – and to his power, protection, provision and so on.

This means that gospel obedience is liberating not restricting – for it keeps us in line with the Father's will, which is always a will for our freedom, wholeness and blessing.

Of course, this sort of 'particular' obedience is only possible when we start to know the Father personally, to recognise his voice and understand his thinking. We examine this in *Listening to God*.

The Scriptures introduce God and provide basic guidelines for every aspect of life. Disciples need to study the whole Bible to grasp God's self-revelation – and to understand how he wants them to live.

No self-justification

The spiritual counterpart of starting to obey God is stopping justifying ourselves. New disciples need to be encouraged to admit to God, to each other, and to themselves, that they are grievous sinners whose only hope is to trust Jesus totally as their personal Saviour.

True disciples do not go about trying to justify themselves, or seeking to make up for their sins by good behaviour, religious devotion or obedience to God's commandments. Instead, they obey God personally in gratitude for the gift of forgiveness which they have already unwrapped – not in a vain attempt to earn forgiveness.

Walk in the Spirit

A third basic step of discipleship is learning to walk in the Spirit. New disciples need to be taught to allow the Spirit to live his life through them; to let him make them more like Jesus; and to learn from him how to apply the principles of God's Word to each situation they face.

Real disciples do not try harder in their own strength to be good, for this is a waste of time. Instead, they depend consciously on the Spirit to do his good through them. They allow him to develop his fruit in their lives, and gradually grow towards perfection as a result of their reliance on him. We consider this in *Knowing the Spirit*.

Start to worship

The final basic step is learning to worship. New disciples need to be taught to express their love of God. They do this not only by singing praises, but also by developing their talents and by doing all their ordinary day-to-day tasks to the best of their ability, and by offering them as a fragrant offering to God. We study this in *Worship in Spirit and Truth*.

All disciples need to learn how to create spaces in their lives when they can worship God more intimately, and draw sustenance and light from him – so that they can shine in the world with *his* light and love.

In fact, we can say that disciples are a little bit like the moon, which is quite dead by itself but shines in the darkness with the reflected light of the sun. The moon is eclipsed when the earth comes between the sun and the moon; and there is spiritual darkness in disciples when the world gets between them and God.

But the sun is eclipsed when the moon gets between the sun and the earth; and there is a similar spiritual darkness on earth when disciples grab the limelight and hinder the passage of light from Jesus to the world – drawing attention to themselves rather than reflecting his glory.

SUBMITTED TO GOD

In *Knowing the Son*, we see that one of the most striking features of Jesus' life is his submission to the Father, and that this is a key secret of his authority. We see this submission in, for example, Matthew 26:39 and 1 Corinthians 15:28.

Matthew 26:39 ☐

1 Corinthians 15:28 ☐

It follows from this that those disciples who want to exercise the same authority as Jesus must first learn to put themselves under God's authority: *we must be what Jesus was, to do what Jesus did.*

A similar principle applies in service. Jesus was wholly dedicated to doing the will of the Father by serving the people among whom he had been placed and to whom he had been sent. It was in doing this that he received all the divine resources which he needed for his mission.

It is the same today. Disciples who want to serve as Jesus served must first submit to God's will as it is expressed in their sociological and geographical setting. They must start by serving the people who are naturally around them, and then they can move on to serve the ones to whom they are clearly sent by God. We must remember that we do not choose where and whom we want to serve!

The Gospels present Jesus as an effective leader of men and women: he called people to follow him, and they willingly obeyed. Jesus' total submission to the Holy Spirit was the secret of his leadership of others – and the same applies to us. Disciples who want to be effective leaders or outstanding examples must first learn to hear and follow the promptings of the Holy Spirit.

For example, Jesus was anointed with the Spirit before the great miracles which revealed his glory; and then, after receiving the Spirit, he prayed and waited in the desert before beginning his ministry.

The apostles followed the same pattern. Jesus breathed the Spirit upon them, but they then had to wait in Jerusalem until they were filled with power from on high. In the same way, modern disciples who want to share God's life and radiate his glory must also submit themselves to God's pattern of receiving his Spirit and patiently waiting for God's right time to minister in power.

SUBMITTED TO PEOPLE

Jesus' submission to other people is, perhaps, the most unexpected feature of his life. In demonstrating the kingdom of heaven, Jesus showed his disciples what it means to be a citizen of earth.

So he meekly submitted to his parents, his cousin John, the weekly synagogue worship, the Romans and Jewish authorities in the payment of taxes, the high priests, Pilate, and the nails of the cross.

As a human, it was in putting himself under human authorities in this way that Jesus gained the right to exercise authority himself. It follows that those disciples who seek to live and minister with Jesus' authority must live as he lived – voluntarily under the authority of others.

Dependence

Jesus also depended on other people. He depended on his parents, his cousin, the women who provided for him financially. He accepted the service of those who accompanied him on his journeys. He stayed with people who wanted to look after him. He valued the friendship and companionship of the disciples – especially the inner three. And he needed Simon of Cyrene to carry his cross for him.

Jesus' dependence on others, as well as on the Father and the Spirit, reveals a basic principle of Christian service. Disciples who want to give must be willing to receive; those who want to minister must be able to accept help; and those who want to serve must depend at all times on other people for the support and resources they need.

This important principle applies in many other areas of discipleship. We cannot become effective leaders of people until we have learned to follow other men and women. Even apostles must always remain disciples – they must never stop learning, following, listening and receiving from other people.

And disciples cannot offer God's love to the world unless they have first received it through other Christians. God may pour his love into our lives by the Spirit, but he usually involves a human partner in the process. Discipleship involves learning to receive God's truth and love from other disciples so that we can pass them on to the world.

ANOINTED WITH THE SPIRIT

Jesus did not submit just for the sake of submitting. He submitted so that he could exercise authority, serve sacrificially, lead with perfection, and reveal God's glory. But submission alone was not enough: Jesus had to be anointed with the Spirit as well.

It is the same today. The anointing with the Spirit is given to enable submitting disciples to live with Jesus' effectiveness – though none of us manages to live with his consistency as people filled with the Spirit.

In *Knowing the Spirit*, we see that God saturates disciples with the Spirit for a host of purposes. For example, his holy anointing equips us with kingdom authority over sickness and evil powers; it empowers us to proclaim the gospel with divine effectiveness; and it introduces us to a life of service which follows the example of Jesus' own life.

When Jesus was anointed with the Spirit at his baptism, God underlined the link between the Spirit and sacrificial service in two clear ways. He inspired John to introduce Jesus as the Lamb of God, and he sent the Spirit in the shape of a dove.

The Lamb implied that Jesus was anointed to be the greatest sufferer of all time. The dove pointed both to Jonah (the name means dove) whose service involved great suffering, and to sacrifice (the dove was an alternative offering for Jews too *poor* to afford a lamb or goat).

Most importantly, God anoints disciples with his Spirit to help them live a life which is moving towards perfection, and to enable them to understand people with the understanding and sympathy of Christ.

The Spirit is the *parakletos*, the one who is called alongside, and he calls disciples to get close to those with whom they have little in common, or even profoundly disagree. He is the 'Counsellor', so any anointing with him is bound to help disciples bring God's counsel to people. And he is the 'Comforter', so he naturally helps disciples to comfort and encourage people, even those they do not especially like.

The Spirit lives to give glory to God, so the disciples' anointing enables us to radiate God's love, to shine with his truth and love, to display more and more of his glory, to focus all attention on him.

The Spirit-filled life

In 2 Timothy 1:7, the apostle Paul highlights several characteristics which should start to develop in every Spirit-filled disciple.

2 Timothy 1:7 ☐

Disciples should not be timid. When Jesus was arrested, his disciples forsook him and fled; but a great change occurred after Pentecost. No matter how much they were flogged or imprisoned, they never stopped proclaiming the good news about Jesus.

Many disciples are naturally shy and reserved: the Spirit's anointing does not turn them into extroverts, it merely enables them to overcome their timidity and embarrassment and tell their friends about Jesus.

Disciples should be filled with *the Spirit's power*. (The Greek word is *dunamis*, from which we derive 'dynamite'.) This is not a divine blast of destruction, it is a constant enabling to defeat and dismiss Satan, to stand in the face of ridicule and persecution, to overcome fear and speak about Jesus, to do the mighty works of God. This enabling power does not stem from natural enthusiasm or strength of character; it comes only from the all-powerful Spirit – and every new disciple needs to be helped to receive his strength.

Disciples should be dominated by *the Spirit's love*. When he comes upon them, they should begin to love God as they have never loved him before. They should find that their hearts are enlarged towards other Christians – even those with different temperaments and from unfamiliar traditions – and towards the hurting people of the world.

Again, this is not natural human love, it is God's personal love which is poured into our hearts by the Holy Spirit. It is the kind of love which goes on loving however discouraging the response or reaction.

And disciples should be characterised by *the Spirit's self-control* or self-discipline. This is the hallmark of the servant spirit which enables disciples to deny themselves in the service of God and people.

Paul showed these qualities of discipleship in his evangelistic work, and in his many sufferings for the gospel, and he attributed them to the work of the Holy Spirit in his life. It is absolutely critical that the Spirit is proclaimed in the good news, so that every new disciple knows the importance of opening themselves to him and seeking his anointing.

SACRIFICIAL DISCIPLESHIP

Luke 9:23 ☐

The call to discipleship is not something which God makes only at the start of the Christian life, for he is always calling all his disciples to a more definite discipleship – and this always involves sacrifice. Passages like Luke 9:23 show that there can never be real Christian effectiveness without a real element of sacrificial discipleship.

So God calls the new subjects of his kingdom to sacrifice their proud self-will, and to learn to obey and submit – so that Jesus may exercise his heavenly authority through them. He orders his subjects to obey:

- *the commands in his Word so that they can live in the kosmos by the authority of his Word*

- *the promptings of his Spirit so that they can rule over evil and sickness in the power of the Spirit*

- *one another in his church so that they can serve with his authority in the church*

- *social structures so that they can establish his kingdom on earth*

God calls his new servants to sacrifice their proud self-reliance, to learn to depend and to accept help – in order that Jesus may serve more effectively through them. He tells his servants to depend on:

- *the promises of his Word so that they can serve in the world according to the demanding standards of his Word*

- *the leading of the Spirit so that they can serve the hurting in the power of the Spirit*

- *other believers so that they can serve one another in the church*

- *the society in which they have been placed so that they can serve the people around them*

God calls his new friends to sacrifice their proud self-confidence, to learn to follow an example in order that Jesus may use their lives as an example to inspire others. He calls his friends to welcome:

- *his example in the Word so that they can demonstrate Jesus' likeness to the world*

- *his encouragements from the Spirit so that they can encourage others to be like him*

- *his correction through one another in the church so that they can bear with one another in the church*

- *everything that is good in society so that they can show his standards and approval in their local community*

And God also calls his new sons and daughters to sacrifice their proud self-centredness, to learn to worship and to accept eternal life in order that they might demonstrate God's eternal nature. He longs for his children to receive:

- *Jesus as the Son of God who is revealed in the Word so that they can proclaim his eternal truth to the world*

- *the anointing of the Spirit so that they can shine with his eternal light in the world's dark places*

- *his love through one another in the church so that they can enjoy his divine love with one another in the church*

- *insights about the nature of life from his creation so that they can care with his love for every aspect of creation*

All new Christians need encouragement and teaching to grasp the full breadth and depth of discipleship. Many churches stress some of these elements, but we need to help people to embrace the whole lot.

UNITED IN THE CHURCH

Whenever a new believer comes to Jesus and begins to trust in him, a brand-new relationship starts – not only with God, but also with all other Christians in the universal church.

Ephesians 2:15–16 shows that Jesus' death united Jews and Gentiles, making one entity out of two, and that the great purpose of the cross was to create a single New Person through-and-for reconciliation. This means that every disciple has a personal relationship with God *and* is organically united with all other believers in the universal church.

We consider the essential corporate nature of the church in *Glory in the Church*, and study passages like 1 Peter 2:9; 1 Corinthians 1:2; 3:9–17; 2 Corinthians 11:2 and Ephesians 1:23.

These passages show that disciples are those who have been carefully chosen from all other people to be the beloved bride of God's Son. He really has chosen us. His Word cannot be broken. His love never fails. And we, the chosen bride, will share the Son's inheritance of all things.

1 Peter 2:9 was originally written for disciples who were facing persecution, for people who were likely to be asked to serve Jesus by

Ephesians
2:15–16 ☐

1 Peter 2:9 ☐

1 Corinthians
1:2 ☐
3:9–17 ☐

2 Corinthians
11:2 ☐

Ephesians 1:23 ☐

1 Peter 2:9 ☐

laying down their lives. So Peter called them a royal priesthood, to show that they were serving the king by sacrificially serving the king's people in all sorts of ways. They were filling themselves, God's holy temple, with the priestly sacrifices of praise, prayer and thanksgiving.

In any country with a monarchy, it is considered a high privilege to serve the royal family in their royal palace; so it must be an incalculable honour to serve the King of kings – even if it does involve martyrdom. Somehow, we need to communicate this high sense of honour and privilege to all new believers.

Disciples also form a holy nation. This means that we have been set apart for a corporate life of dedication and consecration. Paul's favourite image of the church, 'the body', shows that disciples have been re-created into the body of Christ so that he can carry on living his perfect life on earth through them.

And disciples are people who belong to God: we are his church, citizens of his heaven and children of his kingdom. We are subject to God's laws and directed by his Spirit. Quite simply, we are the Lord's.

Prepared for service

We have seen in Ephesians 4:12 that all church leaders are called primarily to prepare the whole church for service. In *Ministry in the Spirit*, we see that the Greek word which is used here, *diakonia*, means practical, menial, lowly, foot-washing service.

Ephesians 4:12 ☐

Every individual disciple is meant to serve God, other disciples and the world, but church leaders are meant to ensure that the church as a whole is characterised by this sort of humble service.

In summary, we can say that the chief purpose of discipleship is to build disciples together in the church and to equip them to serve together in the world. In our proclamation of the good news, we need to announce a full-rounded discipleship which remembers that God wants all disciples, his whole beloved church:

- *to demonstrate that Jesus is the King of kings by obeying his Word, acting with his authority, and relying on his name*

- *to show that Jesus is the Saviour of the world by depending on his death, serving with his effectiveness, and relying on his blood*

- *to make it plain that Jesus is the ideal human by following in his footsteps, leading with his perfection and imitating his example*

- *to reveal that Jesus is the true God by sharing his life, shining with his light, speaking with his truth and showing his love*

Christian discipleship will be delightful – it will be genuine gospel good news – when the church starts to live and serve like this. There really will be glory in the church, and the whole *kosmos* will be filled with the glory of God, as the waters cover the sea. For nothing attracts people more to God, nothing has more evangelistic impact, than lives which are truly Christ-like.

PART EIGHT

evangelism and the spirit

Although the full title of the fifth book of the New Testament is 'the Acts of the Apostles', it would probably be more accurate to call it, 'the Acts of the Spirit through the Apostles'.

The book of Acts opens with a nervous group of about 120 uneducated disciples huddling to pray in a private room; yet it goes on to describe how they became a body of powerful witnesses who overcame fierce opposition and vicious persecution to establish a flourishing church throughout the Roman Empire.

The great power of God can be seen on every page of Acts, as people are healed, delivered, converted, empowered and transformed into credible witnesses of the risen Christ. And the power of the Holy Spirit is always the main reason for the disciples' effectiveness.

There are over fifty references to the Spirit in Acts – 1:2, 5, 8, 16; 2:4, 17–18, 33, 38; 4:8, 31; 5:3, 9, 32; 6:3, 5, 10; 7:51, 55; 8:15, 17–19, 29, 39; 9:17, 31; 10:19, 38, 44–47; 11:12, 15–16, 24, 28; 13:2, 4, 9, 52; 15:8, 28; 16:6–7; 17:16; 18:5, 25; 19:2, 6, 21; 20:22–23, 28; 21:4, 11; 28:25. A careful reading of these passages underlines the vital link between biblical evangelism and the Holy Spirit.

THE SPIRIT AND WITNESS

In *Knowing the Spirit*, we see that witness is the essence of the Holy Spirit. John 15:26–27 shows that the Spirit's two great purposes are:

- *to testify about Jesus*

- *to help us to bear witness to Jesus*

John 16:8–11 reveals the Spirit's calling to convict the world of:

- *sin*

- *righteousness*

- *judgement*

And Acts 1:8 promises that the Spirit's anointing results in:

- *disciples becoming powerful witnesses*

In *Knowing the Spirit*, we establish that the Spirit always brings decisive change. He wants to fill us with power, to help us become pure, to direct us to perform Jesus' work, and to enable us to live in his presence, and he wants to do all this *so that we can know Jesus better and make him better known.*

All these great works of the Spirit, however, relate to his primary purpose of witness. We have noted, in Luke 4:18, that Jesus claimed he had been anointed with the Spirit to evangelise the hurting. And we see exactly the same purpose behind anointing throughout the rest of the New Testament – whenever people are filled or anointed with the Holy Spirit, effective evangelism soon starts to take place.

Passages like Acts 2:41–47; 4:31–33; 6:10; 9:17–28; 10:44–46; 13:9–12; 19:6–20; 1 Thessalonians 1:5–8; Hebrews 2:4; 1 Peter 1:12 show that magnifying God and witnessing to Jesus were the natural consequence of groups or individuals receiving the Holy Spirit.

We can say that the urge to evangelise was bred into the church by the Spirit. At Pentecost, the church became a naturally witnessing church because the continually witnessing Spirit had come upon it. We see this in passages like Acts 4:20.

In fact, the New Testament implies that, whenever the Spirit is present in power, the evangelistic work of the church flows naturally, spontaneously and effectively.

Acts 5:28 shows that, from Pentecost onwards, evangelism just happened. Yet, as we have noted, it happened without any apostolic encouragements or exhortations to 'go and spread the gospel'. Even Acts 11 and 15, which record the early church's debates about the gospel and the Gentiles, do not refer to the Great Commission; instead, they merely mention the Spirit's work, and report that the church was encouraged to acknowledge his work.

Acts 5:28 ☐

Acts 11 ☐
15 ☐

This is both important and relevant. Local churches do not need more calls to mission, more exhortations to evangelise, more reminders of the Great Commission, more instruction in evangelistic techniques; instead, they just need more of the Witnessing Spirit. His anointing will transform any church into an effective witnessing community.

We must never forget that it is utterly useless to attempt to reach the lost, to spread the gospel, or to attempt any form of evangelism, without his presence, his directing and his unlimited power.

THE SPIRIT AND POWER

At first sight, it might appear that disciples who had healed the sick, cast out demons, accompanied Jesus for three years and seen physical proof of his resurrection would be more than adequately equipped to be witnesses. This was not so.

They possessed experience, training and knowledge, but lacked the only acceptable qualification – God's own power, the power of the Holy Spirit. In Luke 24:48–49 and Acts 1:4–8, Jesus promised that the anointing with the Spirit would remedy this deficiency.

Luke 24:48–49 ☐

Acts 1:4–8 ☐

The three thousand people who were converted at Pentecost were the result of the Spirit's power flowing through the 120 disciples. But Pentecost was only the beginning; as we go through Acts, we can trace how the gospel was spread by the Spirit's power. Acts 4:33; 6:8 and 10:38 illustrate the centrality of his power in the church's witness.

Acts 4:33 ☐
6:8 ☐
10:38 ☐

The usual Greek word for power is *dunamis*: this points to an energy which changes everything. It is the supernatural enabling power of God by which miracles occur, witnessing is made effective, and disciples are strengthened to endure persecution and adversity.

The New Testament shows that the Spirit's *dunamis* power has a wide variety of applications. For example, the New Testament reveals that God's power enables disciples:

- *to be a witness to Jesus* – Acts 1:8

- *to witness to Jesus' resurrection* – Acts 4:33

- *to do great wonders and signs* – Acts 6:8

- *to do good and heal* – Acts 10:38

- *to abound in hope* – Romans 15:13

- *to perform mighty signs and wonders* – Romans 15:18–19

- *to speak and preach* – 1 Corinthians 2:4–5

- *to endure difficulties* – 2 Corinthians 6:6–10

- *to rejoice in weakness* – 2 Corinthians 12:9

- *to be strengthened to know God's love* – Ephesians 3:16

- *to stand against the enemy in prayer* – Ephesians 6:10–18

- *to announce the gospel* – Philippians 4:10–15; 1 Thessalonians 1:5

- *to be patient* – Colossians 1:11

- *to share in Christ's sufferings* – 2 Timothy 1:8

Power to proclaim

In the Old Testament, the Spirit's anointing gave the prophets the power to receive, understand and speak God's thoughts. By the Spirit, they knew what God wanted them to say and they had his *dunamis* to say it in public.

In the New Testament, the Holy Spirit still enabled all anointed believers to know what to say and to speak it with a power that they did not naturally possess. We see this in 1 Corinthians 2:4.

Acts 2:4 shows that, when the disciples were filled with the Holy Spirit, the Spirit gave them 'utterance'. This is the Greek word *apophthengomai* which is used only here and in Acts 2:14 and 26:25.

Apophthengomai literally means 'to speak forth' and carries the idea of making a statement in public – which can be seen in 2:14 and 26:25.

This means that the 'utterance' in Acts 2:4 was a specific Spirit-imparted enabling to speak to people: it was the 'get-up-and-go' to testify to other people about Jesus – and this enabling to witness verbally is given *to all believers* who are filled with the Holy Spirit.

Acts 2:4 ☐

Power for miracles

Throughout this *Sword of the Spirit* series, we stress the relevance of the Old Testament prophets. People like Moses, Elijah and Elisha – who had been anointed with the Spirit – found that God empowered their public speaking, and that he also worked miracles through them.

It is the same in the New Testament. Matthew 21:11, 46; Mark 6:4–15; Luke 7:11–17 and John 7:40 show the people assumed that Jesus was a prophet because of the miracles. They recognised that the signs and wonders meant God was with Jesus in a special way, and they assumed that he must be another Spirit-anointed prophet.

Matthew 21:11 ☐
21:46 ☐
Mark 6:4–15 ☐
Luke 7:11–17 ☐
John 7:40 ☐

Acts 6:8 shows that this enabling power was the key to Stephen's miracles. And Romans 15:18–19 underlines that a disciple's miracle-working enabling is always the power of God's Spirit.

Acts 6:8 ☐
Romans
15:18–19 ☐

It is important we remember that the Spirit gives power for miracles essentially in the context of evangelism. In the New Testament, signs and wonders are mainly given to convince people that the message about Jesus is true.

Of course, God also heals because he cares about sick people, but the context is essentially evangelistic – even when believers are healed.

In Acts, miracles have a key role in evangelism. For example:

- *After the lame man was healed, Peter and John were imprisoned and reprimanded, but many of those who had heard Peter's explanation of the miracle became believers.*

Acts 3:11–4:4 ☐

- *The consequence of Saul's healing was his Damascus preaching which led on into his fruitful future.*

Acts 9:17–27 ☐

- *When Aeneas was healed 'everybody who lived in Lydda and Sharon saw him, and they were all converted to the Lord'.*

Acts 9:32–35 ☐

- *The whole of Joppa heard about Tabitha's resuscitation, 'and many believed in the Lord'.*

Acts 9:36–42 ☐

In Acts, effective evangelism is attributed:

- *fourteen times* – to miracles and proclamation together

- *six times* – to miracles alone

- *one time* – to proclamation alone (this was at Corinth – though 1 Corinthians 1:17 and 2:14 suggest that rather more happened there than Luke records in Acts 18!)

This underlines what we establish in *Ministry in the Spirit*, that a right and natural context of healing is alongside the proclamation of the good news. We see this, for example, in Romans 15:18–19.

Few of the people healed in the New Testament were followers of Christ at the time. Paul, Lazarus and Tabitha were disciples; and, probably, so too were Aeneas, Eutychus and Peter's mother-in-law.

The other thirty-two people whom the New Testament describes as being healed by the Spirit's power do not appear to have been believers at their healing. This underlines the idea that evangelism is the main context in which the Spirit chooses to work with powerful miracles.

Power for warfare

Ephesians 6:10–20 and 1 Peter 5:8 show that all Christians are involved in a struggle with the forces of darkness. We can feel weak and inadequate when we think about all the evil and suffering in the world, or when we struggle with some regular personal temptation, or when we try to answer people's objections to our faith. But passages like 2 Corinthians 10:4–6 promise that the Spirit gives us all the power we need for this sort of spiritual warfare.

The Spirit does not enable us just to proclaim the gospel in words and demonstrate it in deeds, he also enables us to live victoriously for Jesus. He provides us with the ability to do what we know we ought to do, and sincerely want to do, yet lack the strength.

He gives us the power to say 'no' to cravings for whatever 'the world, the flesh and the devil' seem to be offering – whether obvious vices like addictions, or less obvious vices like ambition and adulation. And he gives us his enabling to be patient with people, to keep our tempers, to stand firm under pressure, to love the unlovable – in fact, to do all the things that the enemy tries to ensure that we do not do.

Romans 15:18–19

Ephesians 6:10–20

1 Peter 5:8

2 Corinthians 10:4–6

The ordinary problems of life can seem overwhelming, but God gives us his grace and his *dunamis* so that we can overcome our weaknesses and troubles. 2 Corinthians 12:9–10 helps us to put our problems into perspective and to think about them biblically.

2 Corinthians
12:9–10 ☐

Time and again in evangelism, we have to cry to God, begging him to help us, to strengthen us, to give us power to speak and act in the right way, to make us equal to the pressures we face. We can be sure that the Spirit's enabling power is all we need to endure and overcome.

Paul's prayer for *dunamis*, in Ephesians 3:16, should be our constant prayer – both for ourselves and for those whom we love and serve. We desperately need the Spirit's enabling power to help us push back the frontiers of evil in society, to reach the lost with the good news, and to establish God's kingdom in our locality.

Ephesians 3:16 ☐

Power for perseverance

Most believers know some of God's promises. But we need the Spirit's power to translate these into a tangible experience which fills us with joyful hope in the face of disappointment and discouragement. We need to keep praying Paul's Romans 15:13 intercession for each other.

Romans 15:13 ☐

2 Corinthians 6:3–10 and Colossians 1:11 help us appreciate Paul's attitude to difficult circumstances. He knew the truth that God gives patience and grace to endure troubles. We need to remember – and to teach – that the gift of God's *dunamis* for endurance is often God's way for us to overcome hardship and apathy.

2 Corinthians
6:3–10 ☐

Colossians 1:11 ☐

It is the power of the humble Spirit which stiffens our resolve to persevere when the going gets tough. It is the *Parakletos* who urges us to keep going in adversity.

Power for witness

When we try to understand why the Spirit gives his enabling power, we have to consider verses like Acts 4:33. The Spirit gives us power to proclaim and to persevere, for miracles and warfare, in order that we will be powerful witnesses to the risen Lord Jesus.

Acts 4:33 ☐

Miracles are not given to thrill and encourage *us* (though they do). Victory and hope are not given to make *our* lives more bearable (though they do). Instead, they are given essentially to provide an eloquent and effective testimony for *the lost*.

Every aspect of the Spirit's enabling is given to enable us to know Jesus better *and* to make him better known to the lost and hurting world. The real test of true spiritual power is simply whether or not it brings people into a deeper knowledge and understanding of Jesus.

This means that we should talk about the Spirit's work in Christ-centred words rather than human-centred phrases – as if God's power were something which is made available for *us* to switch on and *use*. We must make it plain that we make ourselves available to him, and he uses us; it is never the other way around.

In evangelism, we must take care not to offer the Spirit as some sort of impersonal power which unbelievers can harness and control once they commit themselves to Christ. God's power does not immediately cancel our character defects and make our lives comfortable and straightforward. Our lives are a continuous fight against the pressures and strategies of the world, the flesh and the devil.

Of course, the truth is that the Spirit does bring breathtaking changes through his *dunamis* power. And he does provide us with the strength and ability to do what we know we ought to do. This empowering from Christ through the Spirit is a glorious truth which we should want to experience more and more.

But the Spirit does not over-ride our free will, force us to obey him, or make us speak out. He calls us into a *voluntary* partnership so that we *may* know Jesus better, and *may* reveal him more clearly. The Spirit's power is given, but it is given to turn us into better witnesses, into people whose words and lives – whose everyday behaviour and spiritual authority – effectively reach the lost with the gospel of Christ.

THE SPIRIT AND TRUTH

John 15:26 ☐
16:13 ☐

In John 15:26 and 16:13, Jesus teaches about 'the Spirit of truth'. This shows that the Holy Spirit is more concerned with spiritual truth than spiritual experience, with the truth of God's Word rather than the thrill of God's deeds.

This *Sword of the Spirit* series is a School of Ministry in 'the Word and the Spirit', and we stress repeatedly that the Spirit and the Word go together and must not be separated. Jesus' teaching about the Spirit in John 14–16 reveals that it is the Spirit of truth who abides with disciples, bears witness to Jesus and convicts the world of sin. It is only by being the personification of truth that he accomplishes his works of fellowship, witness and conviction.

John 14–16 ☐

Of course, 'truth' in John's Gospel is personal not propositional, it is the person of Jesus not theological ideas about him – we see this in John 1:17; 8:40, 45; 14:6; 18:37. 'True' truth is the eternal reality of Jesus, and the truth – the Word – brings life to all who receive it.

John 1:17 ☐
8:40, 45 ☐
14:6 ☐
18:37 ☐

When evangelism is empowered and directed by the Spirit, truth is paramount. This means that it essentially focuses on Jesus as truth – on his claims, uniqueness, life, death, resurrection, and so on.

It also means, however, that every aspect of evangelism must be truthful and full of integrity. There must be no exaggeration, no manipulation, no ambiguity, no false claims, no pride, no financial pressure, no questionable motives. There must be personal transparency, deep humility, intellectual clarity, an honest grappling with hard issues like suffering, church disunity, scientific theories, other religions, and so on.

If the Spirit of truth is leading us into all truth, we should proclaim the full truth of the gospel, its personal power *and* its intellectual integrity, the wonderful achievements of the cross *and* the hard historical facts of the cross and the resurrection.

THE SPIRIT AND CONVERSION

In *Knowing the Spirit*, *Living Faith*, *Glory in the Church* and *Salvation by Grace*, we stress that conversion – turning to God – is a process rather than a momentary event. It includes regeneration, repentance, faith in Jesus, forgiveness of sins, baptism in water, receiving the Spirit and becoming a vital part of the church.

This process can be condensed into a few minutes, with all aspects occurring nearly simultaneously – as for the converts at Pentecost.

John 3 ☐

Or it can be spread over a lifetime – though God does not want it to take this long!

In John 3, Jesus seems to distinguish between 'seeing' the kingdom in verse 3 and 'entering' the kingdom in verse 5. Verse 3 shows that God gives the gift of spiritual sight when people are born again – when they are regenerated by the Spirit. This is when our eternal destiny changes and we start to see things 'God's way' and develop a desire for spiritual matters.

Verse 5, however, shows that it is God's will not only for us to be enabled to 'see' his kingdom but also for us to 'enter' deeply into it – to taste, enjoy and live in it. It is this entry which creates the possibility (but not the immediate reality) of victory over sin, power in witness, and growth into the likeness of Christ.

Whether we achieve these or not depends on our obedience and continued living in the Spirit, but the possibility does not arise without entry into God's kingdom.

Regeneration – being born again – is entirely the work of the Holy Spirit. He is the regenerator who is actively involved with the world and unbelievers. John 16:8 shows that he convinces the world about sin, righteousness and judgement; and John 3:1–8; Romans 8:1–14 and 1 Corinthians 2:10–14 make it plain that it is simply not possible to become a Christian apart from the work of the Spirit.

John 16:8 ☐
      3:1–8 ☐

Romans 8:1–14 ☐

1 Corinthians
      2:10–14 ☐

Nobody can choose to be regenerated, and nobody can make it happen. Nobody knows when it will occur, and some people are unaware or confused when it is taking place. We just know when it has happened, for we find ourselves believing what we could never believe before. All this is accomplished *by* the Spirit in the way that Jesus describes in John 3:8. It is his work, not ours.

We noted this evangelistic *partnership* with the Spirit in Part One. As the king's heralds, it is our responsibility to reach the lost with the gospel and direct them towards Christ. It is the Spirit's responsibility, however, to create new life and regenerate unbelievers.

Luke 1:16 ☐

Acts 9:35 ☐
      11:21 ☐
      26:18–20 ☐

We have a genuine role in the partnership. Like John the Baptist in Luke 1:16 and Paul in Acts 9:35; 11:21; 26:18–20, we have been sent into the world so that the lost may turn from darkness to light and from Satan to God.

But, like the first Christians, we cannot do this without the Spirit's power. We should spread the good news in absolute dependence on the Spirit, who alone can open the eyes of the spiritually blind, unstop the ears of the spiritually deaf, warm the hearts of the spiritually cold, and humble the spiritually proud.

Ephesians 2:1 shows that people remain spiritually dead unless the Spirit brings life; and 1 Corinthians 2:4–5 reveals that, without a clear demonstration of the Spirit, the faith of those who believe rests on human wisdom rather than God's power.

Ephesians 2:1 ☐

1 Corinthians 2:4–5 ☐

It is a true partnership, for the Spirit depends as much on us as we do on him. We cannot convert anyone, and he chooses to draw people to Christ through disciples.

If the Spirit worked alone in conversion, there would be little for us to do except pray. But, because he works through disciples, we must work hard at our contribution to ensure that our words, deeds and lives are relevant, credible and Christ-like.

THE SPIRIT AND GUIDANCE

The book of Acts records how the evangelism of the early church was guided and directed by the Holy Spirit, and we consider this throughout *Listening to God*.

Although every revelation from God is essentially a self-revelation about God, and we listen to him primarily to deepen our relationship with him, God does speak to us through the Spirit: he reveals what he is doing so that we can keep in step with him.

As heralds, we are called to pass on the gospel generally to all the people around us. This means that much of our guidance is thoroughly *natural*.

When Paul reached Thessalonica, Acts 17:2 reports that he went straight to the synagogue 'as was his custom' and spent three weeks arguing with them from the Scriptures about Jesus. Paul did not need special guidance from the Spirit to go to the obvious place where he would meet people who believed in God.

Acts 17:2 ☐

Acts 3:1–4:4 ☐

Acts 8:26–39 ☐
    9:10–19 ☐
    10:1–16 ☐
    13:2 ☐
    16:6–10 ☐

Luke 5:1–11 ☐

And Acts 3:1–4:4 describes how several thousand people were converted as a result of Peter and John sharing the gospel with a needy person on their way to a regular prayer meeting.

The Spirit does, however, sometimes guide disciples in a *super-natural* way – through visions, prophecy and spiritual gifts. We see this, for example in Acts 8:26–39; 9:10–19; 10:1–16; 13:2 and 16:6–10. We consider this thoroughly in *Listening to God*.

And the Spirit's guidance is often *corporate*. Although Peter and Paul had received personal guidance about taking the gospel to Gentiles, they submitted their understanding to the whole church at Jerusalem. We see a similar practice in Acts 13:2: Paul and Barnabas had already been called to a work by the Spirit, but they did not act on this until the whole church at Antioch had been guided together.

Jesus taught Peter a very important lesson about evangelistic guidance when he first called him to be a disciple. Luke 5:1–11 contrasts Peter's unsuccessful fishing (which was based on his considerable knowledge of the lake and his vast experience of fishing) with his amazing success when he followed Jesus' guidance.

Many people work endlessly at evangelism in their own strength and experience; but – like Peter – they would be far more effective fishers of men and women if they spent more time listening to God, learning God's particular will, and obeying it completely. It is the work of the Spirit to reveal God's particular will to us – and then, wonderfully, he equips us with everything we need to carry it out.

PART NINE

evangelism and prayer

We know that we are called to depend, consciously and completely, on God in every aspect of our lives. Whenever we do not depend on him, we are bound to rely on ourselves – and that is the way to ruin.

Depending on God involves prayer. As heralds, we are sent into a hostile world with the gospel; and our evangelism always involves powerful spiritual warfare, for the god of this world lies behind all the apathy that we face. 2 Corinthians 4:4 teaches that he blinds unbelievers' minds so that they cannot see the light of the gospel.

2 Corinthians 4:4 ☐

Whenever we urge people to turn to God, we battle with invisible demonic beings. Paul makes this plain throughout Ephesians 6. In 6:18, after encouraging us to put on God's armour, Paul shows that prayer is the chief purpose of the armour. Prayer is not another piece of armour, or else Paul's analogy has broken down. Prayer enables us to use God's armour, for prayer is our spiritual battlefield.

Ephesians 6:18 ☐

In Isaiah 59:15–19, the Lord was so appalled that there was nobody to intercede that he decided to intervene himself; but, before he interceded, he put on his personal armour – and this is the divine armour which the Spirit provides for us when we pray in the Spirit.

Isaiah 59:15–19 ☐

Ephesians
        6:19–20 ☐

2 Corinthians
        10:3–5 ☐

Paul goes on, in 6:19–20, to ask his readers to use the armour and wrestle in prayer *so that he could proclaim the gospel boldly*. He knew that it was foolish to try to evangelise without supporting prayer which was Spirit-inspired, Spirit-enabled, Spirit-equipped and Spirit-empowered. 2 Corinthians 10:3–5 underlines the importance of this.

We cannot expect to see the lost become committed disciples without much intercession. Quite simply, we are very unlikely to see the hurting healed and the lost rescued without persistent, prevailing prayer. We consider this throughout *Effective Prayer*.

EVANGELISTIC PRAYING

The New Testament reveals that the apostle Paul was a tremendous man of prayer, and his letters are filled with prayers for his readers, requests for prayers by his readers, as well as teaching about prayer. The Scriptures also show that Paul was passionate about evangelism – so we should not be surprised to find that most of his recorded prayer requests and prayers were made to facilitate effective evangelism.

Romans 10:1 ☐

Romans 10:1 describes Paul's dearest wish for the Jews. This verse teaches nothing about the *content* of his praying; rather, it reveals the *purpose* of his praying. Romans 10:1 encourages fervent evangelistic prayer, but it does not provide us with a model prayer to use.

As we will see, Paul seems to have prayed, and to have requested prayer, for his own ministry by interceding that the obstacles preventing his evangelism would be removed, and that he would be equipped, energised and motivated to witness more effectively.

This suggests that, when we long for someone to be saved, we will wrestle in prayer to bring about their salvation. Like Paul, we will spend long hours praying with the purpose that they will be saved. We will, however, want to find the most effective way of praying to bring about their salvation. Paul's epistles suggest that effective evangelistic prayer often has two distinct elements:

- *prayer for heralds to be motivated, empowered and equipped*

- *prayer for obstacles blocking salvation to be removed*

Prayers for equipping

The apostle Paul often asked for prayer that he would be kept safe in, or rescued from, a situation which was preventing the proclamation of the gospel.

For example, he asked:

- *to be rescued from evil men* – 2 Thessalonians 3:1–2

- *to be rescued from unbelievers* – Romans 15:31

- *to be rescued from a deadly peril* – 2 Corinthians 1:9–11

- *to be kept safe in prison* – Philippians 1:19–20

- *to be released from prison as a special favour* – Philemon 22

- *that a closed door be opened* – Colossians 4:3

In all these verses, Paul asked for prayer so that he could witness more effectively. He did not ask for hostilities to cease, but for safety as he witnessed in the difficulties. This suggests that we should not ask for an easy life in our evangelistic prayers. Instead, we should try to discover what God wants to do in his world. We should concentrate on his work, rather than be side-tracked by surrounding events.

In 2 Thessalonians 3:1–2, Paul requested prayer that his message should be well received by unbelievers. And in Romans 15:30–32 he asked for prayer that his message would prove acceptable to the Jerusalem believers. This is enabling, facilitating prayer.

In Ephesians 6:19–20 and Colossians 4:3–4, Paul asked for prayer for fearless boldness. He wanted to speak the good news as it should be spoken. He knew his normal state was 'fear and trembling' and that boldness did not come naturally to him. If Paul needed prayer for boldness, how much more should this feature in our prayers today?

And, in Romans 15:22–32, Paul requested prayer for the opportunity to travel to Rome. He asked this so that he could take a blessing from Christ to Rome. If God gives us a similar burden for a particular place, we should ask him for a similar opportunity to pass on his message.

These prayer requests offer clear guidelines about praying for the lost. Like Paul, we know that it is God's will for all people to be saved. We do not need to persuade a reluctant God to save them. Instead, we should pray that:

2 Thessalonians
3:1–2 ☐

Romans 15:31 ☐

2 Corinthians
1:9–11 ☐

Philippians
1:19–20 ☐

Philemon 22 ☐

Colossians 4:3 ☐

2 Thessalonians
3:1–2 ☐

Romans
15:30–32 ☐

Ephesians
6:19–20 ☐

Colossians
4:3–4 ☐

Romans
15:22–32 ☐

- *we are strengthened to overcome any imprisoning circumstances which are preventing our witness*

- *we are filled with boldness to speak God's word*

- *we are given opportunities to witness*

- *our words will be empowered by the Spirit and accepted by our listeners*

- *the Spirit will convict our listeners of their sin and need*

If we have a burden for a particular unsaved person or group, one effective way of praying for their salvation is to:

- *listen to God to establish which disciple(s) he wants to use to reach the person or people on our heart*

- *pray specifically and persistently for God to equip the disciple(s) and to empower their words with his grace and favour*

Of course, God always honours our sincere motives when we simply pray 'Please save the lost'. Such prayers are never a waste of time – but they can be a rather lazy! God wants us to press on in prayer, to seek his will for a situation, and then to wrestle and pray it into being.

Paul's epistles contain several prayers for the equipping of believers. For example, he prays that:

- *God will give them the particular knowledge that they need* – Ephesians 1:17–18; 3:18; Colossians 1:9–10; Romans 10:1–4; Philemon 6; Philippians 1:9–10

- *God will give them the specific strength that they need* – Ephesians 3:16; Colossians 1:11; 1 Thessalonians 3:13

- *God will fill them with his love* – Ephesians 3:17; Philippians 1:9; 1 Thessalonians 3:12

- *God will make them pure and blameless* – Philippians 1:10; 1 Thessalonians 3:13; Colossians 1:10; 2 Corinthians 13:9

- *they will live in a way which reflects God's character and thoughts* – Colossians 1:10; 2 Thessalonians 1:11

- *they will bear fruit in good works, be active in sharing their faith, and be a revelation of God's glory* – Colossians 1:10; Philemon 6; 2 Thessalonians 1:11–12.

Ephesians
    1:17–18 ☐
    3:16–18 ☐
Colossians
    1:9–11 ☐
Romans 10:1–4 ☐
Philemon 1:6 ☐
Philippians
    1:9–10 ☐
1 Thessalonians
    3:12–13 ☐
2 Corinthians
    13:9 ☐
2 Thessalonians
    1:11–12 ☐

Prayers about obstacles

In *Effective Prayer* and *Ministry in the Spirit*, we see how Jesus took the common Jewish phrase 'to move a mountain' and vested it with new power and application.

This phrase is based in Isaiah 40:1–5, where the prophet was told to prepare the way of the Lord. Among other things, Isaiah had to knock down the mountains of difficulty which were obstructing the wide-scale revelation of the glory of God. 'Mountain-moving' is hinted at in Isaiah 2:11–16 and its counterpart of 'uprooting' is suggested in Lamentations 3:65–66. The idea also appears in Zechariah 4:7.

Isaiah 40:1–5 ☐

Isaiah 2:11–16 ☐

Lamentations 3:65–66 ☐

Zechariah 4:7 ☐

In olden days, when an Eastern monarch wanted to travel to distant parts of his kingdom, he would send a party of men, some six months to a year in advance, to prepare the way. These men would make good the bridges, repair the roads, uproot trees and generally do everything they could to facilitate the easy journeying and arrival of the monarch.

John the Baptist was the preparer of the way of the Lord, and so also were the disciples in Luke 10. They went ahead of Christ in pairs to all the places he was to visit. Jesus taught about removing obstacles to prepare the way for God's Word and glory in Matthew 17:20; Mark 11:22–24 and Luke 17:5–6.

Luke 10 ☐

Matthew 17:20 ☐

Mark 11:22–24 ☐

Luke 17:5–6 ☐

In *Living Faith*, we establish that Mark 11:22 is one of a large group of New Testament verses which refer to God's personal faith, and is best translated as 'have God's faith'.

Matthew 17:20 and Luke 17:5–6 show that we do not need much faith to move mountains in prayer, just the genuine article. And God's personal faith is absolute. He is totally self-confident. He knows that he can achieve whatever he wants to do. No obstacle is too large for him, and effective obstacle-removing prayer is not beyond us – once we have received a speck of his faith.

These three passages suggest that there are five stages to obstacle-removing praying.

1.   *know God's will*

This sort of praying is a waste of time if we are not absolutely certain about God's will. We simply must spend time listening to him receiving *his* identification of the particular obstacles which are preventing the person we're seeking to reach from being saved.

We need to ask the Father which circumstances, factors, people, attitudes, and so on, are preventing the work of God from developing in a person. Each Gospel passage suggests a particular type of obstacle for removal, and we consider these in *Effective Prayer*.

2.   *receive God's faith*

Human faith is insufficient for obstacle-removing prayer, we need the God-given confidence that this will happen. When the Spirit gives us God's faith, we are to accept the obstacle as already removed.

This is the difference between a faint hope that something might take place, for example, 'I believe (but am not really sure) James will come today'; and knowing for certain that it will happen, for example, 'I believe (he has promised me, and there he is walking towards me) James will come today'.

3.   *announce God's order*

The verses do not say 'Whoever prays to me', but 'Whoever speaks to the mountain'. This prayer is addressed to the obstacle, not to the Father. We learn about these 'prophetic announcement' prayers in *Ministry in the Spirit*.

Luke 10:1–16 ☐

This executive authority, which Christ gave to the disciples in Luke 10:1–16, is ours today. This means in practice that, if God reveals the obstacle preventing a person's conversion to be 'David', a cynical colleague, it could be right to intercede *privately* as follows: 'David, in Jesus' name, I command you to stop obstructing the gospel.'

4.   *persevere in prayer*

The Greek tense in these verses means that we are to go on saying to the obstacle, 'Get up and throw yourself in the sea.' It is not a one-off command. As with all prayer, perseverance is required.

5.   *keep praying until there is a visible result*

The construction of the phrases 'it will be done', 'it will move', 'it will obey', emphasises the certainty of fulfilment. Luke uses a Greek tense which refers to a time prior to the command, for example, 'it would have obeyed': this underlines the fact that there will be a *visible* answer to this obstacle-removing prayer.

When we know God's will, receive God's faith, and keep on announcing God's authoritative order, there can be no doubt about the outcome. The highest mountain, the most deeply rooted tree, the most immovable obstacle, all will go. The blind will see, the lost will be found, the way will be made clear for the glory of God.

THE DISCIPLES' ROLE IN PRAYER

Whenever we pray about evangelism – whether for God to motivate and equip his heralds, or for an obstacle to be removed – we need to remember that he has given us several complementary roles in prayer.

For example, we pray as citizens of the kingdom of heaven who are under the authority of the King of kings, and as liberators who are triumphing in Jesus' name. Because Jesus is the rightful ruler of every situation which is brought to God in prayer, we should pray with *authority* – especially with regard to Satan and the forces of evil.

However, we also pray as sick people who have been made whole, as sinners who have been justified, as servants who know that they can pray only because they are supported by the constant intercession of Jesus. There are many times, for example, when we need to be healed before we can offer healing, and need to be forgiven before we can lead someone to repentance. This means that we should pray with *humility* – especially when we are praying for sinners.

We also pray as followers of Jesus, and as examples to others, who are being brought towards perfection by his perfect humanity because we are filled and controlled by his Holy Spirit. When we follow the prompting of the *Parakletos*, we will pray with the compassion, concern and tears of Jesus, and will become more like him in his ability to get alongside hurting people. So we should pray with *sympathy and understanding* – especially for the ordinary problems of life.

And we pray as believers who are ourselves the fruit of Jesus' labour, as people who have received his life, as children who have been born again and adopted into his family. We know that God can do exactly the same work in others, and so can pray with *confidence* – especially for those who seem to be as far from God as we once were.

The concerns of prayer

Over a period of time, it is easy to slip into praying about a few favourite matters, but we all need to try and maintain a well-rounded approach to prayer which covers a wide range of concerns – rather like we see in the Lord's Prayer.

For example, the kingdom should be a major concern of our prayers. We should pray for Jesus to rule every part of our lives, for more believers to obey him fully, and we should claim his complete victory in situations which are not as they should be.

Christian service should be another concern. We should pray for God to meet the needs of the sinful, the sick, the mentally ill, the homeless, the hurting, the unpleasant, and so on. Of course, we do not pass complete responsibility for these matters to God by our intercession, for our prayers about service should include requests for his strength to serve the needs that we have been given the resources to meet.

We should also pray about the problems which really concern the lost – debt, social disintegration, unemployment, and so on. And we should pray that we will become more like Jesus, and will increase in understanding, sympathy, patience, friendliness and joy.

Above all else, however, we must be concerned with God himself in our prayers, and should spend time honouring, worshipping and loving him for his sake.

We should want our prayers to be answered so that his name is glorified. We should be concerned to make God proud of his children, and to make Jesus thrilled with his bride. We should be worried that some believers are not anointed with the Spirit, and that others are not living in the fullness of his power. And our prayers should reflect God's distress at the state of his beloved *kosmos*, and at the apathy of so many people towards their Creator and Redeemer.

The content of prayer

Although prayer is essentially Godward in direction, most of our evangelistic prayers are about people, and we need to think carefully about how we should pray for them.

Everybody has an enemy, and our of our chief roles in prayer is to free the bound. On the cross, Jesus broke in principle the power of

Satan over all humanity and in every situation; but it remains for us to claim and apply this victory. We do this in prayer.

Some people whom we are concerned to reach are plainly in the grip of evil, for example, they may be bound to alcohol, drugs or materialism. When we pray for them, we may need to add fasting to our praying. We consider this in *Effective Prayer*.

There are many other situations where the devil is obviously at work. So, sometimes, we will need to pray for a friend to overcome anxiety, or to resist temptation, or to choose righteousness. In prayer, we announce the victory of Jesus, speak words of resistance and rebuke to the devil, and command him to leave the situation.

We all know ways in which our Christian friends are less than perfect. Jesus does not spend time criticising his heralds – and neither should we. Hebrews 7:25 shows that, instead, he prays for them. When we are tempted to criticise others, we should join our intercessions to Jesus' and pray that they will become more effective witnesses.

Hebrews 7:25 ☐

In prayer, we should beg the Holy Spirit to convict a person of their particular sin, and should urge Jesus to overwhelm them with an awareness of the Father's sadness at their attitude or action.

And we all know people who need some sort of healing, whether physical or emotional. Some people have fevers, while others get easily hot under the collar. A few people are paralysed, and others insist that they cannot do anything. One or two people suffer from skin disorders, but many more think that they are a terrible sight. Some people are blind, whereas others think that they are always groping in the dark. Many people are deaf, and even more are convinced that they cannot hear God clearly. A few people are lame, and some just hobble along in their spiritual lives. And Jesus can heal them all, can bring wholeness to them all, can reach them if they are lost, and can release them into the work of evangelism if they are saved.

We should bring them all to Jesus in prayer, and go on interceding for them, as Luke 11:8–10 suggests, until our prayers are answered – however long it takes.

Luke 11:8–10 ☐

We have a Friend who cares deeply about all the hurts of fallen humanity – both generally throughout the world, and particularly in people we know. Whenever we get close to a human friend, we inevitably start to share their concerns. So, as we draw closer to Jesus, we should naturally find ourselves starting to intercede about his concerns for his world.

Our prayers should reflect Jesus' passion for the whole world, his yearning for the new creation, *and* his great love for individual lost men and women.

So we should pray, for example,

- for the starving in Africa, *and* for the man down the road whose right knee is giving him pain

- for nations crippled by unjust debt, *and* for our neighbour's difficult marriage

- for political prisoners the world over, *and* for the woman in the next street whose husband is in prison for theft

- for nations which are riddled with desire for material possessions, *and* for our nephew who is about to start school

- for the millions who worship other gods, *and* for more consecration in our own congregation

- for an end to pollution, deforestation and the arms trade, *and* for the lonely woman by the bus stop who never has a visitor

And, knowing that God is well capable of attending to the needs of 5,000 million different people all at the same time, we confidently leave these matters with him. For, no matter how much we may long to reach the lost and save the world, we know that this is his all-consuming desire, his greatest passion, and his ultimate purpose.

PRAYING FOR THE SPIRIT

We have seen that the one factor which, above all others, released the disciples into effective, spontaneous biblical evangelism was the anointing with the Holy Spirit. There are no limits to what God can do through us when we are truly filled and anointed with his Spirit.

If we are to reach the lost; if we are to proclaim, demonstrate and incarnate the good news; if we are to restore a biblical passion and pattern of evangelism to the church, we need the Holy Spirit more than we need anything else.

We need to learn, therefore, how we can be anointed with the Spirit to evangelise the hurting, how we can be filled with God's power to announce his message, do his deeds and live his life.

Repent

First, we must repent of every known sin. Being filled with the Spirit means asking him to control and direct *every* area of our lives – and we cannot pray for this with faith if there is an aspect of our lives which we will not release to him.

We need to let the Spirit examine us so that he can highlight those aspects of our lives which need to change. Of course, we cannot make ourselves holy; but we can repent of those things which grieve the Spirit and prevent him from filling us completely with his love and power.

Down through the centuries, many church leaders have made it their habit regularly to ask themselves a series of searching questions.

For example, we can ask ourselves:

- *am I consciously or unconsciously creating the impression that I'm better than I really am?*

- *can I be trusted to do what I have promised to do?*

- *am I honest in all my acts and words, or do I exaggerate?*

- *do I pass on to others what has been told to me in confidence?*

- *am I a slave to clothes, habits, work, friends, hobbies?*

- *am I self-conscious, self-pitying or self-justifying?*

- *does the Bible speak to me?*

- *am I enjoying prayer?*

- *is Christ real to me?*

- *am I making time every day for the Word and prayer?*

- *when did I last speak to someone with the intention of winning them to Christ?*

- *am I making genuine contacts with unsaved people and revealing God's glory to them?*

- *do I accept criticism and correction?*

- *am I using my finances faithfully and wisely?*

- *is there anybody I fear, dislike, criticise, resent or ignore? If so, what am I doing about this?*

- *am I being generous with all my resources?*

- *do I dwell on sexually impure thoughts?*

- *am I looking after my body with a healthy diet, much exercise and enough sleep?*

- *am I disobeying God in anything?*

- *do I thank God that I am not like some others?*

- *am I defeated in any part of my life?*

- *am I proud?*

- *do I grumble and complain a lot?*

- *am I willing to serve anonymously?*

- *do I need acclaim and recognition?*

- *am I serving others practically?*

- *do I let people down?*

- *am I genuinely submitted to some other people?*

- *do I rely completely on the Spirit, or do I trust too much in my own judgement, experience and training?*

- *am I consciously listening to God?*

- *do I long for the lost to be reached and the world to be saved?*

If we feel that we have scored 0%, it does not mean that we cannot be filled with the Spirit – for he is a gift of God's grace and not a reward for good behaviour! Instead, the Spirit can use these sorts of questions to show us our particular needs and failings, and to lead us to some specific repentance. Whenever we consciously repent of all our known sins, we take a huge stride towards God and open ourselves afresh to his anointing.

Obey

We need to be willing to obey God *wherever* he may lead us and *however* he chooses to use us.

In the Scriptures, the coming of the Spirit was always accompanied by the arrival of hardship, adversity and opposition. We see this in the Old Testament prophets; we see it in Christ; and we see it in the early church. When the Spirit came upon the disciples at Pentecost, their problems really started!

Soon they were imprisoned, beaten, persecuted, scattered, isolated, stoned, shipwrecked, cold, hungry, thirsty, exhausted and in constant danger. This is what being filled with the Spirit meant for them.

But because they were willing to obey God – whatever price they had to pay in this life – his power and purity were constantly manifested through them.

Many disciples today seem to want the thrill of the power and the glow of the holiness, but not the price of the power and the heat of the holiness. In truth, they do not really want to be completely saturated by the Holy Spirit of the Almighty God.

Hungry and thirsty

In *The Rule of God*, we see that we must be hungry and thirsty for God and for a life of righteousness in his presence.

Praying for more of the Holy Spirit should not be a casual request which we make when we feel like a thrill; it should be a serious prayer which we offer when we so long for God to be glorified in our lives that we are pained by our emptiness and powerlessness.

We are ready to be filled and anointed with the Spirit when we are ravenously hungry for God to be honoured as God, for him to be worshipped and adored, loved and served, followed and obeyed – not only by ourselves, but by the whole world, all the lost.

We may feel weak and inadequate, but Jesus comes to us in his grace and offers himself. His John 7:37–39 promise is absolute: when we finally come to him and start drinking, rivers of life-giving, health-bringing living water begin to flow through us – and on from us to others.

John 7:37–39 ☐

Jesus' promise is made in the present tense, which means that we must go on being thirsty, go on being hungry, keep on coming to Jesus and keep on drinking from him – and the healing river of the Spirit will keep on flowing in-and-through us to the afflicted and hurting.

Right now, Jesus is reigning in heaven. One day, all humanity will bow to him and confess that he is Lord. Until then, however, we have been charged and equipped to reach the lost with the glad news that he is Lord.

Acts 2:32–36 ☐

The first evangelistic message of the Christian era, spoken by Peter at Pentecost in Acts 2:32–36, concluded with the trinitarian news that, 'This Jesus God has raised up, of which we are all witnesses; therefore, being exalted to the right hand of God, and having received from the Father the promise of the Holy Spirit, he poured out this which you now see and hear . . . '

This Holy Spirit, who empowered and enabled Jesus to evangelise the hurting, is all we need to reach the lost. We need him to fill and empower us if our evangelism is to be biblical and effective. We need him to guide and direct us if we are to spread the good news in our locality. We need him to encourage and comfort us if we are to persist when apathy and opposition threaten to overwhelm us. We need him. We need the Holy Spirit.

God has not change his mind. He has not withdrawn his promise. He waits for us, his chosen heralds, to come to Jesus with our obvious need; and he will anoint those who ask him with his Holy Spirit – so that we can be his witnesses, his heralds, wherever he chooses to send us with his holy gospel.

ACTIVITIES for individuals and small groups

evangelism

Before you began studying this book, what was your mental picture of evangelism?

....

....

....

Over the last few years, who have you been trying to reach with the gospel?

....

....

How have you been trying to reach them?

....

....

....

Christian groups and traditions have a variety of ideas about evangelism; what different ideas and emphases have you come across?

....

....

....

What does Luke 4:18–19 suggest about Jesus' understanding of evangelism?

....

....

....

What do Luke 7:18–22 and 8:1–56 teach about evangelism?

....

....

....

....

Mark begins his Gospel with a typical day in Jesus' life. What do we learn about Jesus' 'gospelling' in Mark 1:21–34?

....

....

....

....

Acts identifies Phillip as an evangelist. What does Acts 8:5–13 teach about his evangelism?

....

....

....

....

What do these passages teach about the content and purpose of the gospel?

Matthew 4:23; 9:35; 24:14; Mark 1:1, 14; Acts 20:24; Romans 1:1–3, 9; 2:16; 15:16, 19; 16:25; 2 Corinthians 4:3–4; 11:7; Ephesians 1:13; 6:14; 1 Thessalonians 1:5; 2:2, 9; 2 Thessalonians 1:8; 2:14; 1 Timothy 1:11; 2 Timothy 2:8; 1 Peter 4:17; Revelation 14:6.

....

....

....

....

....

And what do these passages teach about the believer's response and attitude to the gospel?

Matthew 4:23; Mark 1:15; 8:35; Acts 20:24; Romans 1:1, 9, 16; 10:16; 15:16; 1 Corinthians 9:12, 14; 15:1; 2 Corinthians 11:4, 7; Galatians 1:11; 2:2; Philippians 1:5; 4:3; 1 Thessalonians 2:2; 2 Timothy 1:8.

....

....

....

....

....

Biblical evangelism has a particular focus on the 'ptochos' – the hurting or the afflicted. Who are the 'ptochos' near or around you and your church?

....

....

How could you reach them more effectively?

....

....

....

....

What are the key differences between a herald and a church preacher?

....

....

....

What are the qualifications for being a good herald?

....

....

....

What do these passages teach about God's heralds and their message?

Matthew 4:23; 9:35; 10:7; 11:1; 24:14; Mark 1:14, 39; 3:14; 6:12; 16:15–20; Luke 4:19; 8:1; 9:2; Acts 8:5; 9:20; 10:42; 20:25; 28:31; Romans 10:8; 1 Corinthians 9:27; 15:11–12; 2 Corinthians 1:19; Galatians 2:2; 1 Thessalonians 2:9.

....

....

....

....

....

What is God saying to you about being a herald?

....

....

the lost

Matthew 9:35–10:15 provide an overview of all the basic principles of New Testament evangelism. What principles do you learn in the following verses? And how is your church putting each principle into practice?

35 ....

....

36 ....

....

37–38 ....

....

5–6 ....

....

7 ....

....

8 ....

....

9–12 ....

....

What does it mean in the Bible to be lost?

....

....

What do you think this suggests about the after-life for the lost?

....

....

When you read John 3:16, what do you think 'the world' means?

....

....

John's Gospel and epistles focus on God's relationship with the world and the world's response to God. What do these passages teach about the world?

John 1:10 ....

John 3:16 ....

John 3:17 ....

John 4:42 ....

John 9:5 ....

John 11:27 ....

John 1:5; 8:12; 9:5 ....

John 7:7; 8:23 ....

John 12:31; 14:30; 16:11; 1 John 5:19 ....

1 John 2:17 ....

John 1:10; 1 John 3:1 ....

1 John 3:13 ....

1 John 4:1 ....

1 John 4:5 ....

Why does God love the world when it is so influenced by evil and opposed to God's people?

....

....

How does God show his love for the world?

....

....

....

What does Romans 8:19–24 teach about the world?

....

....

How is this relevant to evangelism?

....

....

In Western Europe, we tend to think that we have a separate body, mind and soul; whereas the Bible always considers people to be fully integrated beings. What are the practical consequences in church life and mission of our modern, western view of people?

....

....

....

....

What differences would the integrated view make to evangelism?

....

....

....

....

Where does sin come from?

....

....

Why is God so opposed to sin?

....

....

....

How does sin relate to 'lostness'?

....

....

....

What are the principle worries of the people whom you are trying to reach with the gospel?

....

....

....

....

....

motives for evangelism

What courses and conferences have you attended on evangelism? How have they affected your evangelism?

....
....
....
....

How can your church improve the way it motivates, trains and releases people in evangelism?

....
....
....
....

What would be wrong or unhelpful motives for evangelising?

....
....
....
....

What have been your main reasons for evangelising?

....
....
....
....

What have been your main reasons for not evangelising?

....
....
....
....

The Bible suggests that people are not interested in the gospel because they are spiritually blind. What other factors militate against people responding positively?

....

....

....

....

....

....

How can an awareness of the coming judgement be a positive incentive to spreading the gospel?

....

....

....

....

What is the practical difference between evangelism which is motivated by guilt and duty and evangelism which is motivated by love and mercy?

....

....

....

....

What is the most dramatic transformation that you have seen in a new convert's life?

....

....

....

What are the biggest changes that the gospel has made in your life?

....

....

....

....

How can your experience of these changes help in your evangelism?

....

....

....

In your circle of friends and acquaintances, who seems the most hardened or opposed to Christ? How is God going to reach them? What will they be like when they are a believer?

....

....

....

....

....

How do the ideas of 'lostness' and 'reconciliation' relate to each other?

....

....

....

Which of Jesus' parables teach about 'lostness' and 'reconciliation'? What do they show?

....

....

....

Why is reconciliation central to biblical evangelism?

....

....

....

How can the cross motivate you to more effective mission?

....

....

....

the message of evangelism

Why did Jesus restrict himself to the words that the Father gave him? How did he manage to do this?

....

....

....

....

....

What practical difference should this make to your evangelism? How can you restrict yourself to God's words?

....

....

....

....

Why do some Christians focus more on God as Redeemer than as Creator?

....

....

....

How, practically, can a local church strengthen its proclamation and celebration of God as Creator?

....

....

....

What is the difference between 'human-centred' evangelism and 'God-centred' evangelism?

....

....

....

Other than those mentioned on pages 49 and 50, which Old Testament stories, Psalms and prophecies point forwards to the cross? How do they do this?

....
....
....
....

What do you think Jesus said to Cleopas, in Luke 24, when he explained how it had already been revealed that the Messiah would suffer?

....
....
....
....
....
....

How can a local church ensure that the cross is central to its life and mission?

....
....
....
....
....
....

How can you ensure that your message about the cross is more 'God-centred' than 'human-centred'?

....
....
....
....
....
....

How would you respond to someone who made the following statements?

1. *There's no point in believing the English New Testament because it can't bear any resemblance to what actually happened and was said in the first century.*

....

....

....

....

....

2. *Jesus can't have been that important in the first century or he'd be mentioned in lots of other places than the Bible.*

....

....

....

....

....

3. *I can't take the Bible seriously, all the Gospels contradict each other.*

....

....

....

....

....

4. *The resurrection is a crazy idea – there must be a better explanation of what happened.*

....

....

....

....

....

....

....

In our evangelism, we need to show that Jesus came into the world to reverse all the consequences of humanity's fall in Eden. The Eden fall from grace had many different results, and we need to emphasise these equally when we spread the gospel message.

What were the principle consequences of humanity's first sin?

....

....

....

....

....

....

....

What has been your experience of each of these consequences?

....

....

....

....

....

....

....

What did Jesus do, in his life and through his death, to reverse these consequences?

....

....

....

....

....

....

....

....

....

What has been your experience of each aspect of Jesus' achievements on the cross?

....

....

....

....

....

....

....

....

What would be a simple way of explaining the fullness of the achievements of the cross to an interested non-Christian?

....

....

....

....

....

....

....

....

How would you respond to someone who made the following statements?

1.   *If God is love, he can't be all-powerful or he'd put an end to suffering. And if he's omnipotent he can't be all-loving or he'd deal with suffering. You Christians can't have it both ways; suffering proves that God isn't all-loving and all-powerful.*

....

....

....

....

....

....

2. *Everyone's known for almost a hundred years that life just evolved. Your idea that God created the world is unscientific, out-of-date nonsense.*

....

....

....

....

....

....

3. *What about all the other religions? You Christians can't seriously think that you're right and they're all wrong. You're all following God, you just express it in ways which reflect your culture. If God exists, he'll welcome anyone who tries to serve him.*

....

....

....

....

....

....

....

4. *I know the Bible's been important to people in the past, but we can't take it seriously today. Which God do we worship – the angry one in the Old Testament who slaughters people, or the loving one in the New Testament who loves little children? And you can't really trust a book that's full of stories about talking snakes and donkeys, and people who live in whales and walk on water. Come on, admit it's all too far-fetched.*

....

....

....

....

....

....

....

If the Christian life is built on personal faith in Jesus, and we are calling people to have faith in him, why should we try to make sure that our message is logical and reasonable?

....

....

....

....

....

Whenever Paul spoke about Jesus' death and resurrection, he always related it to his personal experience. Like him, we need to stress that the cross is central to the Scriptures, rooted in history, logical, reasonable and packed with profound truths. But we also need to show that it works, that we have seen the Lord and know him personally.

How can you convincingly explain to people that you know Jesus personally?

....

....

....

....

....

....

Jesus' words and presence always divide people. His claims are so absolute, his commands so authoritative, his teaching so unequivocal, that people are either for him or against him. They either respond to him with a 'Yes', or reject him with a 'No'. There is no 'grey' area.

On the day of Pentecost, at the end of the first evangelistic sermon, the crowd responded with a question, 'What shall we do?' True proclamation of the king's gospel message always demands a human response.

What is the response that we should ask for when we evangelise?

....

....

....

....

....

....

personal evangelism

How do the Gospels teach about personal evangelism?

....

....

Make a list of all the Gospel stories you can remember which describe Jesus ministering to an individual. What was the outcome in each story?

....

....

....

....

....

....

Which of these stories do you relate to most closely? Why is this?

....

....

Make a list of the different settings for Jesus' personal evangelism.

....

....

....

....

....

....

What is your experience of evangelising in these settings?

....

....

....

....

How did Jesus make contact with people?

....

....

How, practically, can you follow his example?

....

....

....

....

How did Jesus arouse the curiosity of Zacchaeus and the Samaritan woman?

....

....

....

What arouses people's spiritual curiosity today?

....

....

....

....

How, practically, can you follow Jesus' example?

....

....

....

....

How did Jesus challenge Zacchaeus and the Samaritan woman?

....

....

....

....

....

Why did he challenge each of them in the way that he did?

. . . .

. . . .

What can you learn from Jesus' example?

. . . .

. . . .

. . . .

. . . .

What were the confusing diversions in the two incidents?

. . . .

. . . .

How did Jesus handle these diversions?

. . . .

. . . .

. . . .

What can you learn from Jesus' example?

. . . .

. . . .

. . . .

. . . .

How did Jesus establish commitment in the lives of Zacchaeus and the Samaritan woman?

. . . .

. . . .

. . . .

What does this mean for your personal evangelism?

. . . .

. . . .

. . . .

. . . .

church evangelism

Why should evangelism not be separated from local churches?

....
....
....

Why should evangelism be central to the lives of local churches?

....
....
....

What part does evangelism play in your local church?

....
....
....

How do Paul's letters urge churches to evangelise?

....
....
....

What do these passages teach us about the early church's proclamation?

Acts 2:40; 8:4, 25; 9:22, 27–29; 10:37; 13:42, 43, 49; 17:2, 13; 18:11; 20:20; 28:23.

....
....
....
....
....
....

In what different ways does your local church 'proclaim' the gospel?

....

....

....

What other ways could your church effectively proclaim the good news?

....

....

....

....

What, for you, is the hardest part of proclaiming the gospel?

....

....

....

How can you overcome this?

....

....

....

What part does 'demonstration' play in your local church's evangelism?

....

....

....

How, practically, can 'proclamation', 'demonstration' and 'incarnation' of the gospel be integrated together in a local church's evangelism?

....

....

....

....

....

....

What can you do to help mobilise all the members of your church in evangelism?

....

....

....

How, practically, could your church building serve your church's evangelistic ministry more usefully and effectively?

....

....

....

....

How could your church's evangelistic meetings be made more attractive and effective?

....

....

....

....

What opportunities exist in your church for developing meaningful relationships?

....

....

....

How, practically, can your church reveal God's passion for people even more clearly?

....

....

....

....

How have you encouraged someone in the last few weeks?

....

....

Who should you be encouraging next?

....

evangelism and discipleship

What do Matthew 28:18–20; Acts 20:20; Colossians 1:28–29 and 1 Thessalonians 2:7–12 teach about the relationship between evangelism and discipleship?

....

....

....

....

....

This book suggests that starting 'gospel obedience', stopping 'self-justification', and learning to 'walk in the Spirit' and 'worship' are the first basic steps of discipleship.

Why are these the first steps? How do they relate to Christ's work on the cross?

....

....

....

....

....

If Jesus had been given 'all authority' on heaven and earth, why was he submitted to the Father in everything?

....

....

....

....

What are the practical implications of being submitted to God in the same way as Jesus?

....

....

....

....

Make a list of the different ways that Jesus submitted to other people.

....

....

....

....

What can you learn from this for your life?

....

....

....

....

What difference has the anointing with the Spirit made to your discipleship?

....

....

....

....

Which of the characteristics of a Spirit-filled disciple listed in 2 Timothy 1:7 is least developed in your life, and which is most developed? Why is this?

....

....

....

What is your experience of helping a new convert become a committed disciple?

....

....

....

....

....

....

....

What are some good ways of helping a new convert become a committed disciple?

....

....

....

....

What have you sacrificed as part of your Christian discipleship?

....

....

....

....

What is your next step in sacrificial discipleship?

....

....

....

....

Why is Christian unity important for effective evangelism?

....

....

....

How, practically, can a local church help new converts to develop genuine relationships within-and-across the whole church?

....

....

....

....

What is the evangelistic purpose behind discipleship?

....

....

....

evangelism and the spirit

What do these passages teach about the relationship between evangelism and the Holy Spirit?

Luke 4:8; 24:48–49; John 3:1–8; 15:26–27; 16:8–11; Acts 1:4–8; 4:33; 6:8; 10:38; Romans 8:1–14; 1 Corinthians 2:10–14

....
....
....
....
....

What do these passages reveal about the Spirit's enabling power? What has been your experience of each aspect of the Spirit's enabling power?

Acts 1:8 ....
....

Acts 4:33 ....
....

Acts 6:8 ....
....

Acts 10:38 ....
....

Romans 15:18–19 ....
....

1 Corinthians 2:4–5 ....
....

2 Corinthians 6:6–10 ....
....

2 Corinthians 12:9 ....
....

Ephesians 3:16 ....

....

Ephesians 6:10 ....

....

Philippians 4:13 ....

....

Colossians 1:11 ....

....

2 Timothy 1:7 ....

....

Which of these aspects of the Spirit's enabling do you most need to seek God for?

....

....

If regeneration is entirely the work of the Holy Spirit, and it is not possible to become a Christian apart from the work of the Spirit, why do we need to evangelise?

....

....

....

....

What is our role in evangelism, and what is the Spirit's role?

....

....

....

....

How, practically, could you work more closely with the Spirit in your evangelism?

....

....

....

....

evangelism and prayer

At the moment, for which particular non-Christians are you praying?

....

....

How and what are you praying for them?

....

....

....

....

....

Which specific believer(s) is most likely to reach them with the gospel?

....

....

What 'equipping' prayers should you offer so that these believers can reach your non-Christians with the gospel?

....

....

....

....

....

What obstacles are preventing these non-Christians from turning to God?

....

....

....

....

How, specifically, should you pray about these obstacles?

....
....
....
....
....

At the moment, how do you think of yourself when you pray? What is your understanding of your main role or ministry in prayer?

....
....
....
....
....

What changes do you think you need to make to your praying?

....
....
....
....

What is the most important lesson you have learnt about evangelism?

....
....
....
....

What is God specifically saying to you about your evangelism?

....
....
....
....
....